Discover Joy in Your Golden Years

Your Roadmap for Success

Dr Ray R. Phillips

Discover Joy in Your Golden Years

by Ray R. Phillips

For information, contact
BDI Publishers, Atlanta, Georgia
bdipublishers@gmail.com

Cover Design and Layout: Tudor Maier
BDI Publishers

BDI
PUBLISHERS

Atlanta, Georgia

ISBN: 978-1-946637-36-9

I dedicate this book to everyone getting ready to retire and to those already retired. Life has formed you into who you are, and you still have so much more to give and impact. Your professional retirement marks the beginning of the best years to come, your Golden Years. May they truly be the best years of your life!

Contents

Acknowledgments

Having spent the last decade of my life either flying commercial airplanes or commuting to work in one, I have come to an interesting conclusion. I firmly believe that if I am given the opportunity to strike up a conversation with any of my fellow passengers, and I truly mean any, they would share something with me that would make my life better, and I hope I would do the same for them. I know this to be true because I have experienced it time and time again!

You see, when we start to realize the value of our time and relationships, we look forward to learning from those around us and in our sphere of influence. I have come to realize that where I am in life is the culmination of all the interactions that have filled the time to season me into who I am, and I continue to grow! Therefore, I wish to acknowledge all those people that have taking time to speak into my life and consequently enrich it. It is because of them; I am able to write this book to encourage you to do the same in the best years yet to come.

You too are the culmination of all the interactions that have made you into who you are, and you have so many meaningful conversations waiting for you in your Golden Years. Retirement is not the finish line, but rather a door into the most impactful years of your life. Thus, I especially acknowledge you, the reader, for picking up this book that will undoubtably enable you to Discover Joy in Your Golden Years, and more importantly, make a significant impact in the lives around you! Thank you for being you!

INTRODUCTION:

Discover Joy in Retirement

Ken sits in his favorite La-Z-Boy, sipping his coffee and reading the day's news on his iPad. It's the dawn of another day of retirement, and Ken is living life as the "master of his destiny!" After 40 years in the workplace, raising a family, and progressing through "the ranks," Ken and his wife have reached the retirement finish line and are enjoying the fruits of their labor. Now, they both can live a life of leisure, playing golf, traveling, and spending quality time with friends and family.

The retirement honeymoon started off with great excitement and anticipation. Ken had arrived at a retirement utopia by waking up without an alarm, choosing his own schedule and to-do list, and enjoying the pure bliss of doing nothing. Everything had finally worked out the way all those who had retired before him said they would! The only stressors in his life were not getting the desired golf tee time, conflicting doctor's appointments, and the never-ending "to-do" list of household chores and upkeep.

When his friends and family asked about being bored in retirement, Ken often exclaimed, "I have never been so busy!" He was not kidding. There was always something he could be doing, and it felt like there were multiple competing interests for his time. The first six months of the retirement honeymoon were everything Ken and his wife had expected and more. These were all the things he had worked so hard for. Or were they?

The Dilemma

As time passed and the retirement routine solidified, Ken began feeling anxious and a bit unsettled. For most of his life, Ken found his identity in his work and role as a father and husband. Now that his days of working and raising young children were behind him, Ken felt unsure of himself. He wondered if he was truly ready for this phase of life. He and his wife were still happily married, but this new retirement role meant they would need to find new interests and manage the art of "full-time togetherness."

One day, while sitting in his office paying the monthly bills, Ken noticed his college yearbook and decided to reminisce over the years gone by. As he flipped the pages, he thought to himself, "Wow, how we all have changed since those pictures were taken!" He remembered how focused and driven he had been in those college years, looking toward the future with dreams of limitless opportunities. As he closed the yearbook, he asked himself, "Am I still relevant? What is my purpose? And where do I go from here?"

It seemed ironic to Ken that he had felt a clear sense of purpose during college despite not knowing what the future held. Now, after completing a successful professional career, raising a family, and meeting all his financial retirement goals, Ken felt a strange sense of emptiness. He started wondering if he had retired too soon or perhaps hadn't completely thought through this next phase of life. Unlike his youthful optimism, which had made him feel certain things would work out, he now felt uneasy and unsure of how he would make the most of the time he had left. After spending a few minutes dwelling in self-pity, he channeled the purpose-driven young man from his college days, grabbed an old journal, found a blank page, and penned at the top, "Finding My Way Ahead."

The Transformation

For the first time in over six months, the alarm clock went off at 6:30 am. As he had done for 40 years, Ken silenced the alarm, kissed his wife on the forehead, and headed to the kitchen to start the coffee. This morning, he felt a spring in his step and a sense of excitement for what the day might bring. Ken thought to himself, "Today is the first day of the rest of my life!"

As was his routine, Ken sat in the La-Z-Boy and sipped on his coffee. Normally, he would reach for his iPad and begin reading the news, but this morning, he decided to open the journal he had started the day before. He wanted to reflect on the way ahead in retirement and put those thoughts on the page. As was his nature when trying to figure out a solution to a problem, Ken grabbed a piece of paper, wrote the problem at the top, and let his stream of consciousness flow from his mind and onto the paper.

Here were his thoughts:

What is my purpose?	Why am I here?
Am I relevant?	Who am I?
Do I matter?	Am I hopeful?
Am I growing?	How can I be better?
What challenges me?	What frustrates me?
Do I make a difference?	What am I missing?

Almost immediately, Ken's previous feeling of emptiness was replaced with a focus on re-discovering himself in this new phase of life, and he had not even begun answering any of these questions! Perhaps retirement wasn't the finish line in life but rather a new beginning as he faced uncharted territory. He may not have yet known the answers to those questions he just wrote down in his journal, but he believed the answers might provide some clues for how to make the most of his golden years.

The Benefits

The 6:30 am alarm became the routine, as did the coffee and journal time. Ken realized that he had never really spent time thinking about these questions. His previous work life answered many of them for him or at least distracted him from considering them. Now, he had the chance to re-discover who he was and find a new purpose in his life!

This special morning routine became a spark in Ken's life as he reflected and responded to these questions by writing his thoughts in the journal. Throughout the day, thoughts and ideas would come to him, and he would return to what he had written and modify it as he saw fit. Curiosity and excitement about mapping out his new future replaced his previous feelings of uncertainty and emptiness. The excitement he had felt in those college years had returned, and he was determined to make good on his path.

As he wrote down his answers, Ken realized he had never been in a better position in his life to affect change both personally and relationally. If he could imagine it, he believed he could do it! His quest to learn more about himself and how to leverage his life experiences facilitated his desire to realize a new purpose in his golden years by making the most of each day. The very same benefits can be true for you as well.

Welcome to your Discover Joy in Your Golden Years journey! Congratulations on making your financial goals a reality and finding this book that will guide you toward creating your personalized "Roadmap for Success in the Golden Years." Specifically, this book will help you:

- Discover "Who" You Are (Your principles, values and character)

- Realize Your Continued Purpose (Leveraging your life's experiences and expertise)

- Set Goals for Continued Growth (Visualizing, committing, and realizing positive change)

- Realize Your Potential by Wisely Investing Your Time and Choices

- Visualize Your Lasting Impact: Personal and Relational

The Process: How to Make This Book Work for You

You are about to embark on a journey similar to Ken's, with the benefit of some professional and friendly guidance from someone who has been exactly where you are. This book has a straightforward process to help you get the most out of your golden years. Here's a quick guide to making the most out of this workbook:

1. Read each chapter until you arrive at a set of numbered questions.

2. If you are using this book for your Journal Entries, the titles, sections, and questions are already provided for you. If you are using your own journal, create the same titles, sections, and questions. If you are reading this via eBook or would just like to download a separate journal, you can access that via my website: rphillips@c2eusa.com

3. Answer the questions using a stream of consciousness. Let the answers flow from you without putting too much thought or concern into how they sound. Throw all the grammar rules out the window! Get the ideas on paper as they come into your mind–there will be time to go back and edit them later.

4. Let your journal responses sit for a few days after you answer a set of questions. Then, go back, re-read, and make any amendments or edits as you see fit.

5. At the end of chapters 1 and 2, you will summarize your responses to allow you to easily go back to these sections for reference or refinement.

6. Chapters 3 through 5 build on the foundations established in the first two chapters so these summaries will be very important to help guide you through the development of your personalized roadmap for success.

7. Finally, if you use this book to capture your Journal thoughts and would like to have all your responses transferred to a personalized journal, I will discuss how we could do that for you at the end of the book.

By following this process and building your personalized roadmap through your Discover Joy in Your Golden Years Journal, you will realize and define who you are, specifically your principles, values, and character. You can use that knowledge to leverage your life experiences and expertise to identify and realize your continued purpose in your day-to-day life by filling the voids where you can make a difference. New goals and aspirations will expand your perceived potential, allowing you to visualize and realize a lasting impact that will replace perceived boredom.

Your professional retirement is not the finish line but instead the start line for the best years to come, your golden years. Everything you have done to this point, all the successes and failures, has prepared you for this amazing opportunity! Consider your Discover Joy in Your Golden Years Journal as the starting point to the next exciting phase of life, as well as a treasured memoir of your golden years that you can hand down to future generations when they are ready to embark on their own retirement journey.

Are you excited about what the next stage of life will bring? There's no reason to wait a second longer! Grab your favorite coffee mug, journal, pen, and consciousness, and let's start this process with step one: **Discovering "Who" You Are!**

CHAPTER 1:

Discovering Who You Are

Ashley was getting ready for her economics class when her phone rang unexpectedly. It was her dad, Brian, calling from Bahrain. He had recently retired from the FAA as an Air Traffic Controller with over 32 years of service. After about six months of playing golf, working on projects around the house, and living a life of leisure, he had the idea of putting in a pool in the backyard where the family could enjoy leisurely summer afternoons. By taking a contract Air Traffic Controller job in Bahrain for six months, he could simultaneously return to doing his life's work and pay for a new pool.

When Ashley answered the phone, she was surprised to hear her dad greeting her with a sorrowful tone. Instead of asking how her day was, he apologized for being so busy with work as she grew up. The reflective time away from family and familiarity made him realize he had missed a lot due to work while she was growing up. He felt lost now, not knowing who he was or which direction to go. Forced to retire at 56 years old, his family grown and on their own, he faced the inevitable, yet often unplanned, question: "What's next?"

Brian initially thought he was going to Bahrain to make some extra money for the backyard pool. However, he soon realized a greater purpose during this 6-month period away from home—finding himself and direction for the upcoming "golden years" facing him.

Feeling better after speaking with his daughter, Brian hung up the phone. Then, he grabbed his journal and wrote down the following questions:

- Who am I?
- What is my purpose?
- What do I still want to accomplish?
- Can I still make a difference?

From that moment on, Brian was committed to answering each of these questions. He set aside time every day for journaling, reflecting on the past to chart his path for the future. His initial loneliness and sadness were replaced with a renewed sense of connectedness and excitement for where this point in his life had led him and what was still in store in the years ahead.

Those six months ended up flying by. When Brian finally returned home, he not only had the money for a new pool but also a better idea of who he was and where his life was taking him. He realized that the 32 years he had spent as an air traffic controller made him well-suited to serve in his community as a volunteer missions' planner at his church. His ability to multitask, communicate, problem-solve, and build teams made him the perfect choice.

More importantly, serving in this role gave Brian the daily satisfaction he had become accustomed to. He realized he could provide these same skills to his family and relationships by deliberately investing his time and talents. Finally, the daily reflection and journalling he had started in Bahrain became permanent habits in his continuing quest to become and grow into who God created him to be.

It seems ironic that you spend your formative years figuring out which path to choose, what your values are, and how you are defined. Without fully understanding your principles, values, and character, you enter the workplace, conforming to policies and procedures that shape your identity. The focus shifts from understanding yourself to being defined by your profession. Your answer to the casual dinner party question, "So, what do you do?" becomes the categorical definition of who you are in society's eyes, and you spend the next 30+ years refining that definition.

On top of that, you enter relationships and start families that further define your identity, masking and distracting you from your quest to understand who you are at that moment and who you are becoming. Does this sound familiar? The reality of this description is that it is the typical progression of life. It highlights that you are ever-evolving, growing, and becoming, often without really knowing who you are. Perhaps this is why Brian felt lost, unsure of who he was, and unable to answer the new question he was asked at dinner parties, "What's next?"

Discovering Who You Are is the first milestone to Discover Joy in Your Golden Years and developing your personalized roadmap for success. Retirement affords you the opportunity to finish the natural quest to determine who you are and realize the joy of being you! By understanding what guides your choices and behaviors (**Principles**), what is essential in life (**Values**), and who you have become and wish to become (**Character**), you can discover who you are.

Principles

Merriam-Webster defines principle as "a kind of rule, belief, or idea that guides you. In general, a principle is some kind of basic truth that helps you with your life." One of my principles in life is making the most of the day I have been given and appreciating it even when it may not have turned out how I planned. It can fall into the "easier said than done" category, especially on the days that test me the most. I'll tell you about one of those days.

As a 25-year-old Air Force Pilot, I was flying a mission transporting important cargo to a Navy base in Washington State. We had departed Texas with a planned fuel stop in Arizona. When we landed for that fuel stop, the Ground Controller relayed a message that I was to call back to Texas once I got into base operations. This request was unusual, so I rushed to make that call once I could. On the other end of the phone was my commanding officer, who relayed that my 50-year-old mother was in a coma, and I needed to get to the hospital as soon as possible.

I received additional information as I traveled. My mother, who was diagnosed with breast cancer when I was in high school, was once again fighting the disease. This time, it had spread throughout her lymph nodes. The nemesis I had thought she had fought off for good was back with a vengeance.

When I got to the hospital, my mom was lying in a hospital bed on a respirator. The doctors told us in hushed tones that she was "fighting to stay alive." I softly held my mom's warm hand and told her I was there and that I loved her. To my and the doctor's surprise, she squeezed my hand in acknowledgment. It signified to me that my mom fought hard to stay alive so that she could have this last time together. As hard as it was, I told her that we would all be ok and that if she needed to go home to heaven, we would be alright. She must have heard me because she took her last breath shortly after that conversation.

That was the hardest thing I have ever had to say up to that point in my life. I knew that life without my mom would never be the same. As I sat in that small hospital room that somehow smelled simultaneously of disinfectant and my childhood memories on a day that had begun just like any other, I realized just how much of a gift each moment is. I vowed to my mother's memory that I would carry that lesson with me for the rest of my life.

My experience of losing my mother exemplifies how the principles in life that guide us can be very deeply rooted. Scientific studies suggest that genetics determine 20-60% of our temperament; the other 80-40% comes from our life experiences. The temperament or personality we are born with is impacted by those events that shape our lives, and the most significant learning occurs during adversity or mistakes. A 1999 article in Neuroscience, "Learning from Mistakes," suggests that "active synaptic connections are temporarily tagged and subsequently depressed if the resulting output turns out to be unsuccessful."[1] In other words, when things don't work out as we desire or plan, our brains note it.

Witnessing my mother's passing and being there with her right up until the end instilled the principle of living each day to the fullest in me. It was a principle I didn't have up until that moment. Maybe you're different. Perhaps you already live by an established set of principles. If not, consider what significant events have changed your life. What circumstances or situations can cause you to well up with emotion and reflect deeply on someone or something? The answers to these questions will provide insights

---

1 Chialvo, D. R. & Bak P. (1999). Learning from mistakes. Neuroscience, 90(4), 1137.

into who you are on the inside and the principles you are already being guided by.

Another way to think about this is by asking, what guides your life now that you are not defined by your profession? Here are a few "timeless principles" that you can use as a jumping-off point:

- Do unto others as you would have them do unto you
- Think of others more important than yourself
- Listen more than you speak
- Believe in something
- Be kind to your neighbors
- Take care of your health
- Let your actions speak louder than your words
- Treat others the way they want to be treated (Platinum Rule)

This limited list of principles highlights only a few guidelines that have proven to conform to society's policies and procedures for getting by over time. Now, let's dig deeper by asking some more meaningful questions to uncover your principle(s).

1. Which personal guidelines/rules are non-negotiable for you and why?

   What are some rules you will abide by no matter what? What is it about that rule that makes it non-negotiable? Is it because of your faith or belief system? Have life lessons taught you the hard way through mistakes and the school of hard knocks? It could be that your upbringing during your formative years or the identity you gained during your work years have formed the rules that guide you.

2. Which guiding rules do you follow that make you *you*?

   Over the last five or so decades, your life has painted a portrait of successes and failures, joys and hardships, and expectations and disappointments that reflect your beauty! Yes, I said beauty because each of those representations has made you into the beautiful person you are. The first step in discovering who you are is honestly assessing your life to this point, not by reflecting on those representations but by looking within yourself at what makes you who you are.

3. What are your passions?

Another critical insight into discovering who you are is finding out what you are passionate about. What things get you out of bed early in the morning and keep you up late at night? What are those things you do that "just feel right?" Where do you find peace and solitude? These are important questions because they tap into what makes you who you are, and ironically, they provide insight into the principles that guide your life.

For example, I am passionate about people. I love seeing others succeed. I happily will get up early and stay up late, given the opportunity to speak and encourage others. I am passionate about writing this book to encourage those getting ready to retire or those already retired to experience their golden years as the best years of their lives! By spending deliberate and focused time reflecting on what guides you and your life, those principles, if you will, you are taking the first step towards finishing the job from your formative years to figure out who you are.

I have posed many questions throughout this first discussion on Principles, and it is critical that you take the time to reflect and answer them. So, now is an excellent time to begin your "Discover Joy in Your Golden Years" journal, just as Brian did in Bahrain. As you read this book, the practical roadmap you will develop will be tailored directly to you as you journal your thoughts and answer the posed questions. Each chapter will build upon the previous, and you will have the roadmap you desire when you reach the conclusions.

Let's begin your journaling:

Journal Chapter 1

"Discovering Who I Am."

Principles

Again, when you initially answer these questions, try not to think too deeply about each one but rather write down what comes to mind first. Allow that stream of consciousness to flow freely onto your journal pages and resist the urge to re-read or edit your thoughts.

1. What rules, beliefs, or ideas currently guide your life? (List 3)

_____

_____

_____

_____

_____

_____

2. What "timeless principles" do you live by? (List 3)

_____

_____

_____

_____

_____

_____

3. What significant events have shaped your life and the way you live it? (<u>List 2</u>)

_____

_____

_____

_____

_____

4. What are you passionate about? (<u>List 3</u>)

_____

_____

_____

_____

Let these answers sit for a few days. If other thoughts come to mind, create an "Other Thoughts" section and jot them down.

<u>Other thoughts:</u> (List the other "streams of consciousness" here that come to mind).

_____

_____

_____

_____

After about a week, review everything you have written above summing up your thoughts into 3 or 4 principles you live by. As an example, here are the Principles I Live By:

- Make the most of every day regardless of the circumstances

- Think of others more important than yourself

- Begin with the end in mind (Covey)

- Attitude is everything

Principles You Live By: (List 3 or 4)

_____

_____

_____

_____

_____

When you reach this point, you will have crossed the threshold of beginning to understand what guides your choices and behaviors. Now, let's look at what defines you and your **Values** by deciding what is essential in your life.

Values

Roger Federer is considered by many to be the Greatest of All Time (GOAT) tennis player. With 20 Grand Slam titles, 103 ATP titles, 28 ATP Masters 1000 titles, and two Olympic medals, he stayed the world's Number 1 player for 310 weeks. After a 25-year career, at the age of 42, Roger retired from the game he so dearly loved to be the father and husband life had prepared him to be. The poise, demeanor, elegance, and grace he had refined on the tennis court would now be well-suited for his new role.

The value of all his hard work and preparation would now be replaced by new relationships, more family time, and travel on his schedule. Through introspection, Roger realized that the time was right to move on to a new phase of life, one that would draw him closer to the relationships and interests he valued and now had time for.

The concept of value is a fascinating discussion that changes at different times in life. Your values evolve as you evolve and are often subjective, personal, and emotional. For instance, in your youth, you likely valued security, friends, and acceptance. As young adults, you valued education, opportunity, and freedom. In your adult years, we are more likely to value relationships, recognition, and purpose.

Along the way, life challenged you with success and failure, new births and unexpected deaths, and a clear realization that there is very little you can control. These life realizations refine your values to those things that really matter–things like family, relationships, good health, and safe communities. As you climbed the ladder of success, you tried to balance those things that really mattered with work obligations. But once those work obligations go away, what is the plan to address and fully invest in the things you value?

Where you primarily focused outward in determining the principles that guide your life, defining your values requires looking inward to those things that are foundational to your identity or personality. In a sense, those things you value define who you are.

Here's another way to think about your values – how would you define your personality to someone who didn't know you? The words you would use are likely tied to your values.

In his book, *The Nature of Human Values*, Psychologist Milton Rokeach proposed a list of two sets of values: Instrumental Values and Terminal Values.[2]

---

2 Rokeach, M. (1973). *The Nature of Human Values*. Free Press.

Instrumental Values (preferable modes of behavior)	Terminal Values (desirable end-states of existence)
Ambitious (Hard-working, aspiring)	A world at Peace (free of war and conflict)
Broadminded (Open-minded)	Family Security (taking care of loved ones)
Capable (Competent, effective)	
Cheerful (Lighthearted, joyful)	Freedom (Independence, free choice)
Clean (Neat, tidy)	Equality (brotherhood, equal opportunity for all)
Courageous (Standing up for beliefs)	Self-respect (self-esteem)
Forgiving (Willing to pardon others)	Happiness (contentedness)
Helpful (Working for the welfare of others)	Wisdom (a mature understanding of life)
Honest (Sincere, truthful)	National Security (protection from attack)
Imaginative (Daring, creative)	Salvation (saved, eternal life)
Independent (Self-reliant, self-sufficient)	True Friendship (close companionship)
Intellectual (Intelligent, reflective)	Sense of accomplishment (lasting contribution)
Logical (Consistent, rational)	Inner Harmony (freedom from inner conflict)
Loving (Affectionate, tender)	Comfortable life (a prosperous life)
	Mature love (sexual and spiritual intimacy)
Obedient (Dutiful, respectful)	
Polite (Courteous, well-mannered)	Obedient (Dutiful, respectful)
	Pleasure (an enjoyable leisurely life)
Responsible (Dependable, reliable)	Social recognition (respect, admiration)
Self-controlled (Restrained, self-discipline)	An exciting life (a stimulating active life)

Looking at this list, which Instrumental and Terminal Values resonate with you? Are there any of these values you may have had in the past that are no longer yours? Are there any of these values that have been with you for as long as you can remember? Finally, which of these values would someone who knows you well attribute to you (even if you might not do so yourself)? Feel free to jot your answers down now in your journal or just keep them in mind until the end of this section.

As I look at myself, I attribute Ambitious, Cheerful, Forgiving, Independent, and Responsible as my Instrumental Values to achieve Family Security, Self-Respect, Salvation, Sense of accomplishment, and Social Recognition as Terminal Values. These values become insightful as the "lenses through which we view the decisions we make."[3] Translated into my values, when life throws me a curveball or setback, I choose responsibility, seeking a cheerful response that will sustain my self-respect and family security to hopefully provide a sense of accomplishment. I have long wondered why I consistently "looked for the bright side," perhaps to a fault. When I realized that one of my life's principles has been "to make the most of each day," it made sense to me that I would choose to find the bright side, even if it is through the darkness, because today is all I have; tomorrow is not guaranteed.

Your life experiences influence your principles and values, framing your perspective. Paying attention to how you perceive the world around you is also insightful into understanding who you are and becomes the synthesis of your principles and values. Once you have written down on paper (in your journal) those principles that guide your life, the next section to accomplish is **My Values**, both Terminal and Instrumental.

Just like you did in the Principles section, ask yourself the following questions regarding your values:

<u>My Values</u>

1. What are my Instrumental Values? (Use the Rokeach list above or add your own. List all that apply.)

_____

_____

_____

---

3 Covey, S. (1990). *Principle Centered Leadership*. Fireside.

_____

_____

2. What are my Terminal Values? (Use the Rokeach list above or add your own. List all that apply.)

_____

_____

_____

_____

_____

3. How are these Values in line with the Principles I have previously identified? Provide an example to illustrate.

_____

_____

_____

_____

4. Considering both the Principles and Values you have identified; how would you describe your perspective of the world and your life?

_____

_____

_____

_____

Again, write down what comes to mind in a stream-of-consciousness format. Let it sit for a few days, then refine as you see fit, asking yourself if you are starting to better understand who you are and why you see things the way you do. Remember that Principles guide your decision-making, and Values are the lenses through which you view those decisions in terms of importance.

The last step in discovering who you are is to define who you have become–your **Character**.

Character

Considered a natural wonder, the Grand Canyon is 277 miles long, up to 18 miles wide, and over a mile deep at its deepest point. It averages 4000 feet deep throughout its length. Scientists are not sure as to its age, but there is no doubt that this colorful and magnificent wonder was created by the erosion of the Colorado River. People come from all over the world to gaze upon the unique characteristics of this canyon in awe of the colors, vastness, and sheer beauty of what time has done to this geographical feature.

In the context of our discussion of what has guided our lives (Principles) and what we consider essential (Values), this magnificent wonder was created by the path of the Colorado River, assisted by Mother Nature. Its essential features of granite, schist, limestone, and sandstone reflect its unique personality and beauty. Time and life experiences have crafted it into what makes it a wonder.

So far in your journal, you have hopefully discovered some of the principles you live by as well as values you believe are essential to your life. Given these discoveries, the next logical question is, who have you become? What characteristics define you and your life? How do others describe you? How do those who know you best describe you? How would you describe yourself?

"It has been said that our reputation is how others view us, and our character is who we really are."[4] Take the Grand Canyon as an example. Reading or hearing about it (reputation) is never as meaningful and authentic as viewing it in its natural state (how it really is).

4 Phillips, R. (2021). *Finding Joy in Leadership*. BDI

As you enter or approach retirement, the fact is that your work has not only defined you, but it has also shaped your reputation. Now that you are no longer accountable to workplace policies and procedures, forming the "right impression" should be replaced with demonstrating an authentic impression.

So, how can you characterize yourself to determine what your Character is? Let's try an insightful exercise. From the following "List of Virtues," choose those you believe apply to who you are by placing an **X** next to those virtues. When you are finished, have someone who knows you well, place an **O** next to those virtues they believe apply to you.

Accountability	Joy
Assertiveness	Justice
Character	Kindness
Creativity	Love
Compassion	Loyalty
Confidence	Moderation
Consideration	Patience
Cooperation	Perseverance
Courage	Purposefulness
Detachment	Reliability
Diligence	Resilience
Empathy	Respect
Enthusiasm	Responsibility
Friendliness	Self-Discipline
Forgiveness	Service
Generosity	Trustworthiness
Gratitude	Orderliness
Helpfulness	Unity
Humility	Wisdom
Initiative	Integrity

When considering the list above, I would characterize myself with the following:

Accountability, Compassion, Courage, Diligence, Enthusiasm, Forgiveness, Gratitude, Humility, Integrity, Joy, Perseverance, Responsibility, Trustworthiness, and Wisdom. I then asked my wife of 40 years to characterize me by the same list, and here is what she came up with: Accountability, Character, Compassion, Confidence, Consideration, Cooperation, Friendliness, Forgiveness, Generosity, Humility, Initiative, Integrity, Kindness, Love, Loyalty, Perseverance, Purposefulness, Reliability, Respect, Service, Trustworthiness, and Wisdom.

The common character traits we both listed were Accountability, Compassion, Humility, Integrity, Perseverance, Trustworthiness, and Wisdom. This simple effort illustrates that who we think we are and who others think we are quite frequently differ.

The fact is, determining who you really are requires some serious introspection on each of these Character traits. If you find that the common traits chosen by you and your loved one reveal the person you thought you were, that's great! If not, what are the differences between who you are and who you want to become? Then, what can you do to reconcile the differences? If you can cite multiple examples of habitual actions that support certain character traits, chances are they reflect your Character. Remember, your reputation is how others view you, and your Character is who you really are.

If this exercise reveals that you are still acting the same as you were when you were employed full-time, you are not alone. Having spent the last four decades in the workplace, I have also defined myself by my work, which only affirms where we started in this chapter: "Discovering Who You Are." By taking the time to decide what guides you (Principles), what you consider essential (Values), and now reconciling who you have become by characterizing your virtues (Character), you are well on your way to understanding your uniqueness and who you really are at this point in your life.

Now it's time to finish the first draft of Chapter 1, "Discovering Who I Am." I say draft because "becoming who you are" is a never-ending process while you still live and breathe. Create a "My Character" section in your journal and list those characteristics you would use to define yourself. Then, have someone who knows you well do the same. Put both of those lists within your journal and let them sit for a few days.

My Character

Characteristics I define myself by:

_____

_____

_____

_____

_____

Characteristics others define me by:

_____

_____

_____

_____

_____

When you return, create a reconciled list titled "Who I Have Become." Reconcile the list by affirming habitual actions that support that Character trait.

<u>Who I have Become:</u>

(List the reconciled Characteristics)

_____

_____

_____

_____

_____

Now, summarize **Discovering Who You Are** and write the following:

<u>Discovering Who You Are</u>

"Guided by my principles of (list those you have in your journal) and those things I feel are essential in my life (list your values, narrow them down to 4 or 5), I have become a person characterized by the following: (list your virtues, narrow them down to 4 or 5). This is who I am today and fortunately, this is still a "work in progress."

(Fill in the blanks below with your answers)

"Guided by my principles of _____
and those things I feel are essential in my life _____,
I have become a person characterized by the following: _____
_____. This is
who I am today and fortunately, this is still a "work in progress."

Here is what my summary looks like:

> "Guided by my principles of making the most of each day, thinking of others more important than myself, beginning with the end in mind, and keeping a good attitude along with my values of ambitious, cheerful,

forgiving, and responsible to achieve family security, self-respect, salvation, and a sense of accomplishment, I have become a person characterized by accountability, compassion, courage, encouragement, gratitude, and humility. This is who I am today, and fortunately, this is still a "work in progress."

No different than the ever-changing Grand Canyon, life's experiences will continue to refine and mold you with each experience. What makes the golden years so exciting is that you can chart your own path by first knowing who you are, and then, based on that knowledge, **Realizing Continued Purpose** by deciding how you will use the only two things you have control over: your time and choices.

CHAPTER 2:

Realizing Your Continued Purpose

Twelve members of the 1978 high school graduating class recently met in Mesquite, Nevada, for their annual golf get-together. Whenever this group gets together, they transparently pick up where they left off, whether last year or on graduation day 46 years ago. There is no "posturing" or facades but pure acceptance because they knew each other in those formative years and accepted each other for who they were and who they have become.

What makes this annual high school get-together so remarkable is the therapeutic purity and reinforcement each member gives one another. Many in this year's group are retired or within a few years of retirement. All have been through life's hard times, yet none judge the past. Instead, all accept each other for the goodness they have come to know. The fact that all have failed in some way makes them even more accepting and further tightens the bonds of friendship.

Knowing where you started is critical to understanding where you fit in today. You see, where you "fit in," or what others might describe as "your calling," is what I describe as **Purpose**. This is why the focus of Chapter 1 was discovering who you are and trying to finish the process that started in your earlier years. With a better understanding of your Principles, Values, and Character, you can now shed the posturing and facades you created during your work years and accept yourself for who you have become to realize your continued purpose in your golden years.

While accepting yourself may sound simple, it is the hardest thing you will face as you enter your golden years. You are now faced with answering, "Why am I here?" and "Where do I fit in?" In other words, asking, "What is my purpose?" as you face the accountability of whether your life still matters despite all the challenges that brought you to this point. Without work to define you, you must now discover how best to use your time and talents. And so, your purpose becomes a reflection of the past and a reconciliation for the future.

Life creates so many expectations: education, a successful career, financial freedom, family, good health, travel, lasting friendships, and the list goes on. No one ever makes it clear just how difficult life is. Once you realize that you may not meet all your expectations, disappointment sets in, and the wisdom of not being in control of everything takes root. Yet, the reality is we humans only control two things: how we use our time and the choices we make.

During my senior year in college, my mother (whom I spoke of earlier) placed a note on a birthday card: "Accept me as I am so that I can learn what I can become." At the time, I thought she was providing me insight into her life. Years later, I realized that she was encouraging me to accept life and those within my sphere of influence so that I could make the most of any circumstance life throws my way. In other words, receive the gift of each day and choose to make the most of it!

Realizing your Continued Purpose begins with an assessment of your life to date, asking:

- What is my expertise?
- What unique life experiences have I had?
- Where do I feel like I fit in?
- What life lessons have made me a wiser person?

By **reflecting on your life experiences, observing the world around you,** and responding to where you can **fill the void**, you can realize your continued purpose in your golden years.

Reflecting on Your Life's Experiences

As we discussed in the previous chapter, your life experiences have molded you into who you are. The real question is, "What have you learned along the way?" And perhaps more importantly, "What will you do with that knowledge?"

Answering those questions requires self-reflection, defined as "a deeper form of learning that allows us to retain every aspect of any experience, be it personal or professional—why something took place, what the impact was, whether it should happen again—as opposed to just remembering that it happened."[5] Self-reflection is a form of accountability to yourself, accounting for events and experiences in the past to facilitate growth and wisdom for the future.

My career as a pilot with over 40 years of experience ingrained the practice of self-reflection into my routine. After every flight, I reflected on what went well and what I could have done differently. The conclusion from that reflection was often a note to myself of what I learned, and I would frequently review those notes before the next flight. Based on those reflections, I can attest that I have never flown the "perfect flight." But with reflection, I was able to come pretty close.

In the military, we call that type of self-reflection the "debrief," which is considered the sortie's most crucial part. Similarly, medical doctors are described as "practicing" their professions. Because humans and the science of medicine are ever-evolving, doctors must continuously learn and apply that knowledge to their profession, constantly striving for perfection while accepting they will never achieve it.

Consider the consequences for pilots and medical doctors if they stop learning and reflecting. Stagnation could be lethal in both cases. Regardless of your previous occupation, the same is true as you transition from working to retirement. Life is a continuation of becoming, and we constantly evolve if we stay physically and mentally engaged. Just as you did in your work life, you must stay sharp in retirement to make the most of those golden years.

You cannot know if you are staying "sharp" without a baseline against which to measure. That baseline comes from self-reflection about:

• Significant events that have shaped your life

5 Journaling Tips & Resources, Feb 13, 2023

- Significant relationships
- Who you have become
- Professional Challenges
- Personal Challenges

The single event of losing my mother that I described in Chapter 1 helped me deal with career setbacks, relational challenges, and the loss of other loved ones. Because of that experience, I am equipped with compassion and understanding for those in my sphere of influence when similar events occur. I suspect my passion for seeing others experience joy directly relates to these reflections.

Hopefully, you captured a significant event that shaped your life and have that written in your journal under Principles. As you reflect on your life experiences, keep your journal close by referring to the discovery of who you are; this will help stimulate that reflection and provide a framework to guide you further on the journey of charting your course in retirement.

As I have reflected on my life's relationships, I have realized there is a lot I don't know about many of my relatives. What events shaped their lives? What wisdom did they acquire during their lives that I could learn from? What did they do in their golden years? Were their golden years the best of their lives? Imagine if you could read a personal journal from one of your long-lost relatives that described the events that shaped their life and the challenges they faced along the way. How insightful would that wisdom be to you and your life? Consider how the wisdom you bring to your journal could impact future generations.

Let's continue this process by creating "Chapter 2" in your journal:

Journal Chapter 2

"Realizing Your Continued Purpose"

<u>Reflecting on Your Life's Experiences</u>

Upon Reflection—

1. What experiences have provided a deep sense of learning and growth?

_____

_____

_____

_____

_____

2. What relationships in your life have molded you into who you have become?

_____

_____

_____

_____

3. What professional challenges pushed you beyond your perceived limitations?

_____

_____

_____

_____

4. What personal challenges significantly impacted your current outlook?

_____

_____

_____

_____

_____

5. What unique expertise do you have because of your life experiences and relationships?

_____

_____

_____

_____

Once again, write down what comes to mind and the stream of consciousness generated by reflecting on these questions. Let your written thoughts sit for a few days, then refine them as you see fit. The goal here is to reflect on the lessons learned from the past with an understanding of who you are to move closer to realizing your purpose for the future.

Realizing your purpose in this chapter will involve a needs assessment. Based on reflection, you can now know who you are and the unique expertise and perspectives you possess. You can look outward toward your family, community, and affiliations to see where needs exist that you may be suited to fill and support. In other words, once you have completed this section of your journal, it is time to focus outward and **observe the world around you.**

<u>Observing the World Around You</u>

As an airline pilot, I spend a lot of time in airport terminals watching people. I see families going on vacation and the excitement in their faces. Business travelers use every spare moment to connect to the internet while simultaneously charging their devices. I watch the window washers proudly ensure everyone has a clear view of airplanes taxiing, taking off, and landing. And because I am frequently in uniform, I routinely provide directions and advice.

The overall harmony of people from all walks of life is remarkable, sharing the same space and time without apparent tension or discord. When broken down to the fundamentals, human beings want security, relationships, hope, and opportunity. The beauty of the airport environment is that it takes away the hustle and bustle of day-to-day life and simplifies it into deciding what is essential (what we pack for the trip), what is important (our relationships and security), and the chance for a different perspective (the view from 36,000 feet).

There is no doubt we live in an over-stimulated, fast-paced world. Between the constant noise of media, social media, political division, and daily life, finding peace and avoiding chaos must be a deliberate choice. While you were still in the workplace, you didn't have the time to become consumed by chaos due to the distraction of work. Now that you control your time in retirement, it can be easy to fall into the rabbit holes of distraction. Therefore, it will be critical to develop a daily routine "that is reasonably predictable, helps meet values and goals that give meaning to life, fits with the resources available, and keeps conflicts and disagreements relatively low."[6] In other words, you need to build your personal "airport environment" by focusing on what is essential and providing a meaningful perspective.

As a teenager, I remember listening to my grandparents talk about how bad "everything was" in our country and world. They

6 Weisner, T.S. (2010). Well-being, Chaos, and culture: Sustaining a meaningful daily routine. In G. W. Evans & T.D. Wachs (Eds.), *Chaos and its influence on children's development: An Ecological perspective* (pp. 211-224). *American Psychological Association*

seemed bitter and disappointed about politics, the economy, and the younger generation and suggested that "everything was going to h-ll"! That seemed harsh to me at the time, yet we hear all the same issues and perspectives half a century later! The difference now is the noise levels of this chaos due to the velocity of social media, the internet, and the 24-hour news cycle.

While it's important to stay informed about the events in our communities, country, and the world, it's also essential to be deliberate about when, how, and where you get your information. I'm sure you have heard about the importance of eating a good breakfast to start the day. The same is true about what you put in your mind. Starting the day with what you value in life and "feeding" your thoughts by reading or meditating on something directly aligned with those values will sustain you throughout the day.

How you get information about the world must also be deliberate. Listening to 24-hour news cycles, social media feeds, and multiple news applications has been directly related to anxiety levels. In a 2023 study of 47 students over 14 days, the findings showed statistical significance between social media and news application use and increased anxiety.[7] Thus, getting the information in a single sitting and not listening to the constant cycle is critical to maintaining anxiety levels.

Finally, where you observe the world you live in is also essential. Getting out into your community, exploring your city and state, and traveling to new places are crucial to maintaining a balanced perspective. Just as in the airport, when we get out of our day-to-day chaos and observe the world around us, we come to the comforting conclusion that human beings aren't so different after all; we all want security, relationships, hope, and opportunity.

What we seek, we typically find. If you look for fault in human beings, you are rarely disappointed. If you look for good in human beings, while it may take longer than finding fault, you are always satisfied. We must all be deliberate in how we observe the world around us regarding what we are looking for. Therefore, as you

---

7 Jeevar, V., Reif, S., Bliesener, M. (2023), *Journal of Social Media in Society*, 12(2),

observe the world around you through the lenses of your values, ask yourselves the following questions:

<u>Observing the World Around Me</u>

1. What will you fill your mind with as you start each day that will feed what you value in life?

_____

_____

_____

_____

_____

2. How will you stay informed about what is going on in your community and world without increasing your anxiety and distracting you from what is essential?

_____

_____

_____

_____

_____

3. Where will you go to view your "world" first-hand to enhance your perspective and awareness?

_____

_____

_____

_____

4. What will you seek to find as you observe the world around you?

_____

_____

_____

_____

_____

Once you have responded to this section's questions, read through all that you have written in the journal, validating that your Principles, Values, and Character are in line with self-reflection and recently answered questions. Because each part of this book builds on the previous, they must align toward your destination: Discovering Joy in Your Golden Years.

I mentioned earlier that discovering your purpose is basically a needs assessment. Realizing your unique expertise and experiences while observing the world around you allows you to now see where your skillset fits into the areas around you where you might make a difference. Now, it is time to begin discovering your purpose in retirement by discerning where your expertise and experiences fit in as you observe the world around you and realizing your continued Purpose by **Filling the Void**.

Filling the Void

The Learjet 35 (C-21 Airforce Designation) taxis up to the distinguished visitors ramp at Ramstein Air Base Germany. The jet is 48 feet, 7 inches long, 4.9 feet wide, and 12 feet, 3 inches high. It typically seats 7 passengers, but today, it is configured to carry only 3. The passenger door opens, and a 7-foot-1 inch, 325-pound man emerges onto the tarmac to greet military and civilian fans in support of his USO (United Services Organization) tour for service members.

Raised in a military family, Shaquille O'Neal (Shaq) never forgot what being a military dependent meant to him and his family, and he was genuinely excited about giving back. Having gone to high school in Fulda, Germany, before returning to the United States to finish high school, this visit was as much a homecoming as it was part of a USO tour. Committed to giving back, Shaq has always been searching for his calling and seeing where he might fit in!

Before retiring from a distinguished NBA career in 2011 at the age of 39, Shaq fulfilled his promise to his mother to complete his bachelor's degree in general studies from LSU, followed by an MBA from the University of Phoenix and eventually his Ed. D in Human Resource Development from Barry University in 2012. Shaq always knew there had to be more after retirement, and he would spend the next decade realizing continued purpose.

From sportscasting to "Icy Hot" commercials and franchising to advisory boards, he has used his athletic expertise and his educational prowess to continue contributing. Shaq stepped into the retirement world with enthusiasm and energy, becoming as much of a "retirement MVP" as he was an NBA MVP. I love the quote, "Don't ever peak because the only way to go from there is downhill!" Shaq has yet to peak!

Shaq has shown us that retiring from one phase of life isn't the end – it is just a door to the next phase. Retirement is an opportunity to redefine yourself through new experiences, education, perspective, and growth (which we will discuss in Chapter 3). The active and most rewarding part of this needs assessment, or as we have titled this chapter, "Realizing Your Continued Purpose," is finding the voids just waiting for YOU to fill them.

Your expertise, experience, and life lessons have brought you to this point; now, what do you do? What is the cost of engaging versus not engaging with the world? Relevance is perishable, and out of sight is out of mind. So, how do you remain relevant and meaningful in our world? The answer lies in finding and filling the void.

You have spent the last 40-plus years looking for opportunities to advance within your career niche. For many, staying aware and constantly hungry ends with retirement. You may no longer seek something that provides incentive other than the satisfaction of "meeting a need." Why is that?

Can you only do something good when there is a financial incentive? Or do you have the capacity to find purpose without reward? The choice is yours! Filling the void is not about you but rather YOUR abilities, expertise, and desire to find meaningful participation. Continued Purpose is not as much about your personal or financial fulfillment as it is about "filling" the lives of others.

Joy in Your Golden Years is found in the pull of filling the void with your expertise and experience to help another succeed at your expense. It is the counterintuitive concept of giving more than you receive and being humble enough to find gratitude in the gift. We each seek this Purpose: to affirm who we are, why we are here, and what we will do in these golden years. Your Continued Purpose is what gets you up early in the morning and keeps you up late at night. It satisfies your soul and gives meaning to life. Living it is true Joy!

When Shaq retired from the NBA, he was financially set with endorsements and his investments. He could have spent the rest of his days lounging poolside, secluded away from the world. So why did he get a doctoral degree, engage in new business ventures, develop projects in his hometown of Newark, New Jersey, engage in mixed martial arts, and even professional wrestling? His lifestyle suggests it wasn't because he needed the money.

Instead, it seems he pursued all of those ambitions because he felt a calling to give back and learn more. Maybe he realized there is still more to life than a successful professional career. Perhaps he realized the fact that when you give, you get so much more in return. I saw it in December 2001 when he emerged from that tiny jet with a larger-than-life smile, excited to give to the troops!

Where will you seek to fill the void as you emerge from your life's work and enter that next phase of retirement? Will you fulfill a lifelong commitment by finishing something you promised to do when you had the time? Will you go back to school and learn a new skill? Will you offer your skills and expertise to your community? Filling the void is an action, not a concept.

This action begins with a review of your journal/personal roadmap. Review Chapter 1, validating who you are in the context of your Principles, Values, and Character. Look at the two sections you have created in Chapter 2, which validate your life experiences, expertise, and lessons learned. Return to the idea of observing the world around you and the answers you provided to the questions posed.

Considering all of this, create the final section of this chapter:

Filling the Void

Ask yourself the following questions:

1. What unfulfilled promises (to yourself or others) do you need to make good?

_____

_____

_____

_____

_____

2. Where do you find fulfillment? (In community, relationships, service, or learning)

_____

_____

_____

_____

_____

3. What are the three immediate needs within your sphere of influence? (For example: family, church, neighborhood, community, etc.)

_____

_____

_____

_____

4. How are you suited to support those needs? (what experiences make you uniquely qualified?)

_____

_____

_____

_____

5. Where do you feel a "calling" in your sphere of influence?

_____

_____

_____

_____

_____

As you answer these questions, consider them a contract with yourself. The insights you gain from these answers will provide the beginning of your action plan to Realize Continued Purpose in your golden years.

Just like you did in Chapter 1, bring all of this together in an actionable statement: (to help you I have listed my continued purpose below)

<u>My Continued Purpose</u>

"Reflecting on my life's experiences

_____

(list those life lessons, experiences, and expertise)

and observing the world around me

_____

(list what you will fill your mind with, where you will get your information, where you will go to observe your world, and what you will focus your search on),

I will commit to filling the void by

_____

(list the promises you will fulfill, the three immediate needs you can impact, how you will impact those needs, and your internal calling to fill this void).

<u>An Example of: My Continued Purpose</u>

"Reflecting on my life's experiences of sincere gratitude for the opportunities I have been given as a father, military officer, businessman, and pilot, I am committed to starting each day with an attitude of gratitude, staying informed of the world around me without being consumed with these events, seeking to find good in everything, even the smallest of things. With this attitude, I will serve as a retirement coach, continue to write on Discovering Joy, and expand my circle of like-minded friends."

This is only the beginning, the catalyst of your perpetual journey to becoming and contributing to your golden years. Through this evolution, you will **Set Goals for Continued Growth,** which is the topic of our next chapter.

CHAPTER 3:

Setting Goals for Continued Growth

I t had been sixteen years since the U.S. men's gymnastics team had medaled in the Olympics. As the team competition was winding down, one event was left to determine the outcome: the pommel horse. For the U.S. team, it would all come down to a 25-year-old, self-proclaimed nerd the team had labeled "The Specialist."

Usually, the five spots on a team are assigned to "all-around" gymnasts who compete on each apparatus. Yet, for the 2024 Olympics, the U.S. decided to allot one slot to a "specialist" on the pommel horse: Stephen Nedoroscik. A 2020 electrical engineering graduate from Pennsylvania State University and self-proclaimed nerd, Stephen sat behind his teammates, waiting to compete and secure his team's third place bronze medal.

With his eyes closed, he visualized his entire routine, moving his head as if on the pommel horse competing. Unlike any of his competitors, Stephen wore black-rimmed "Clark Kent" glasses to compensate for a condition called coloboma and strabismus. This condition made his eyes sensitive to light and gave him no depth perception. In fact, it prevented him from having a driver's license.

As his competitors finished up and the crowd responded, Stephen remained focused on visualizing and remaining committed to trusting all the hard work and growth he had put into training in the past and channeling his energy toward executing with excellence. When it was time for him to compete, he shed his warm-up suit and glasses and confidently approached the pommel horse.

The moment Stephen grabbed the rings of the pommel horse, his experienced hands took over. He executed the next 80 seconds with mastery as his teammates wavered between cheering him on and holding their breath. By the time he dismounted, Stephen and the rest of the world knew with certainty that he had succeeded in securing the bronze medal for the men's U.S. Olympic team.

When setting goals and achieving them, there are few better examples than an Olympic athlete, and even more so, one with a disability. Like Stephen's preparation for the Olympics, you have spent your entire life preparing to grab the "handles" of your golden years and demonstrate what all the hard work of the past has prepared you to do in this next phase of life.

In my first book, *Finding Joy in Leadership*, I discussed the importance of writing down your goals for the future, continually referring to them, and keeping them in the forefront of your mind. I found out that by doing that, over 85% of what I had written down came to fruition.[8] Not only did I achieve my goals, but I grew from those achievements.

Now that you have discovered who you are and realized your continued purpose, it is time to consider what your future will look like.

Journal Chapter 3

"Setting Goals for Continued Growth"

Briefly answer each of the following questions:

1. What do my "ideal" Golden Years look like?

_____

_____

_____

_____

_____

8 Phillips, R. (2021). *Finding Joy in Leadership*. BDI.

2. What changes will I make to achieve that ideal (personal and relational)?

_____

_____

_____

_____

_____

3. How will I make those changes?

_____

_____

_____

_____

_____

Your answers are the foundation for realizing continued growth in your golden years.

Setting goals for continued growth (Personal and Relational) requires **visualizing** how you want things to be, **committing to the changes needed** to realize that vision, and **making changes** to ensure you reach those goals.

Visualizing Your Golden Years

Many people underestimate the power of vision. Here's a story to illustrate its impact. Identical twin boys were placed in two separate identical rooms on Christmas morning, one with gifts piled high and the other with horse manure piled just as high. The first twin went into the room full of gifts with great joy and excitement. He opened each gift with great anticipation, placed it aside, and continued the process until all the gifts had been unwrapped and discovered. When the dopamine rush of opening the unknown gifts had worn off, this twin seemed disappointed and saddened.

The second twin was led into the room piled high with horse manure and greeted the opportunity with a huge smile and great anticipation. He climbed to the top of the pile and began searching it by handfuls. Using the time it took the other twin to go through all the gifts as a benchmark, the second twin was interrupted and asked why he was so gleeful. With a big smile, he replied, "I know there is a pony in here somewhere!"

The first twin seemed to have all he could have ever wished for and yet was disappointed. His short-term vision was limited to the anticipation of finding out what was behind the wrapping without any absolute clarity of what he was looking for. The second twin had nothing but a "pure" vision of the horse hidden in the manure and never lost his smile and hope!

The power of vision can't be overstated, yet it is frequently underutilized. Perhaps this is why I suspect over half of all retirees fail to have an actionable plan for retirement. According to an October 2024 study by Newsweek, "around 56% of Americans have no solid plan for their retirement, meaning a large portion of retired people lack a clear idea of how they will spend their time after leaving the workforce."[9] As Benjamin Franklin famously said, "People who fail to plan are planning to fail." If you can't visualize your success, there is a high probability it won't happen!

When Stephen Nedoroscik was sitting behind his teammates before the pommel horse competition, he had to block out all the noise in front of him and visualize each move of his routine, knowing that if he could, he would.

Create a section in your journal titled: "My Vision for the Golden Years." As you eagerly wait to grab the handles of your golden years, ask yourselves the following questions and visualize the answers:

9 Higham, A., (2024, October 31), Half of Americans Have No Retirement Plan: Study, *Newsweek*

<u>My Vision for the Golden Years</u>

1. Knowing who I am and my continued purpose, what do I "see/visualize" in my golden years?

_____

_____

_____

_____

_____

2. As I visualize those golden years, what don't I see that I wish I could?

_____

_____

_____

_____

_____

3. As I visualize those golden years, what do I see that I wish I couldn't?

_____

_____

_____

_____

4. As I visualize my golden years, how do I see them ending?

_____

_____

_____

_____

_____

After reading each question, I invite you to close your eyes and try to picture the "ideal" answer in your mind. When you have that picture, write it down. Do the same for each of the four questions. Again, let the answers sit for a couple of days, and if other "visions" come to mind, capture them in your journal as well.

When you return to review, correlate your answers with your journal to date. Do this by reviewing your journal from the beginning to its current end, asking yourself if there is alignment with your Character, continued Purpose, and Vision for your golden years. As you evaluate this alignment, I hope you will feel the excitement of the realization that your ideal vision is possible!

The next step in setting goals for continued growth is to determine the action steps to make your vision a reality and **commit to the changes** required to get there.

Committing to Change

Peyton Manning is a two-time Super Bowl champion, five-time MVP, and fourteen-time Pro Bowler with the Indianapolis Colts and Denver Broncos. Perhaps not as athletically talented as his younger brother Eli or even his older brother Cooper, what gave Peyton the edge was his unwavering work ethic and ability to visualize excellence and set goals to realize it. When the rest of his teammates retired for the day, Peyton stayed to review game film from previous games, looking for every opportunity to learn and grow. He made it his goal to be the most prepared player on the field.

Visualization is a continuous process of conceptualizing an idea, establishing goals and milestones to realize it, growing from those goals, and visualizing it all over again. Therefore, once you have visualized your objective (in our case, making the golden years the best of our lives), it's time to establish goals, realize the vision, and commit to making the necessary changes. Everything that has led up to this point is relevant, but now is the time for an action plan. There is never a perfect time, but there is always a time to make the next step!

When you answered questions about your vision, you gained insight into the changes you will need to make that could allow you to grow and move forward. This idea is the catalyst that encourages you to set growth goals, write them down, and make them happen. In other words, it's time to "find the pony" and seek unwaveringly to do just that. The vision brought you here, and now you must commit to reaching the "goal post!"

You are likely familiar with the concept of goal-setting from your working years. In contrast to those goals that are focused on achieving some career milestone, setting goals in your golden years should primarily be focused on you and your relationships with others. The real reason for an 85% success rate on setting goals, writing them down, and constantly reviewing them is that YOU define the goals that provide YOU clarity, motivation, measurement, and accountability. So, now it's time for you to write down your goals.

Create a "Committing to the Changes Needed" section in your journal, and answer the following questions. Be very honest with yourself about each one and try to write down _three actionable and measurable steps/goals_ you could make to help you realize each one. Don't overthink your answers; just let the thoughts flow from your conscience.

<u>Committing to the Changes Needed</u>

When considering **personal goals,** ask yourself the following questions:

1. What can you do to improve your physical health?

a) _____

b) _____

c) _____

2. What can you do to improve your mental health?

a) _____

b) _____

c) _____

3. What new skill would you like to learn?

a) _____

b) _____

c) _____

4. What new hobby would you like to take up?

a) _____

b) _____

c) _____

When considering **relational goals**, ask yourself the following questions:

1. What relationships do I need to invest more time in?

a) _____

b) _____

c) _____

2. What new relationships would I like to make?

a) _____

b) _____

c) _____

3. Am I as relatable as I would like to be? How could I be more relatable?

a) _____

b) _____

c) _____

4. Am I positively growing from my current relationships?

a) _____

b) _____

c) _____

After you have answered the questions in these two areas, go back and ask yourself:

- Are these goals realistic and measurable?
- Are these goals specific and achievable?
- What is a reasonable amount of time needed to achieve these goals?

Evaluate each of your stated goals with these three questions. If the answer to the first two questions is YES and the amount of time to achieve them is reasonable, you have successfully identified the changes needed and the ability to commit to them. If not, take some time to reassess your goals and see how you can adjust them.

The last step in setting goals for continued growth is **Making the Change.**

Making the Change

I spent the first four decades of my life as a serious student of leadership and followership. I was constantly intrigued by those organizations that seemed to operate flawlessly compared to those that consistently struggled. At the same time, I became intrigued by marathon running. I ran about 40 miles weekly in training and competed in 4 to 5 marathons a year. All of those miles added up to a lot of extra time to think as I ran.

I often conceptualized ideas for a book but couldn't connect the thoughts beyond a chapter or two. One day, after a run, I shared my frustrations about not being able to finish more than a chapter with my wife. To my surprise, she suggested I go back to school and get my PhD. I must tell you that this was never a thought on my radar, yet the more I thought about it, the more I was challenged by the idea.

Getting a PhD would make me a better writer, thinker, and learner. Although it had been over 30 years since I had been in the classroom, I embraced this growth challenge, which clearly pushed me outside of my comfort zone and positively affected significant changes in my life. The vision of writing the thoughts in my mind could now be realized.

For me, earning a PhD was about more than a degree – it was about the growth that would come along the way. The first step to making changes in your life is a sincere willingness to grow. There is that time-old adage that "you can lead a horse to water, but you can't make them drink." We are all creatures of habit. Those of us on the brink of retirement have been creating those habits for decades. It is so easy to get comfortable with our day-to-day lifestyles and natural to resist changes to that comfort. You have worked your entire life to get to where you are and deserve the perks you can now afford.

The real question is whether those perks enhance or deteriorate our lives. I came up with a mantra several years ago that challenges me with my habits and routines: "The difference between a groove and a rut is only a millimeter." In other words, if you feel like you are in a groove in your life and everything is going your way, be careful not to stagnate, or you could find yourself in a rut and no longer growing.

Before I challenged myself to go back to school, I was in a comfortable rut. I had great ideas and intentions but needed to grow. I needed a way to get into a new groove by following motivational speaker and successful performance coach Jim Rohn's suggestion that "successful people do the necessary things that unsuccessful people are not willing to do."

The point is, if you want things to change, YOU must be willing to change! Discovering Joy in Your Golden Years is all about continued change and growth. It is about believing you can still be anything you want (just as you felt in your formative years). The difference between then and now is that you have many more options based on your experience, expertise, and purpose.

Despite their perceived limitations, Stephen Nedoroscik and Peyton Manning rose to the top of their sports because they were willing to grow and do the necessary things to achieve excellence. We all have limitations, yet we also accommodate those limitations. Ironically, running marathons was the catalyst for overcoming my perceived limitations in writing a book.

Physically challenging myself enhanced my mental abilities as the endorphins released during my runs got the "creative juices" flowing. You can experience the same collateral benefits that will allow you to grow beyond your perceived limitations by being willing to change and try new things.

Create a "Making the Change" section in your journal and address the following questions. Once complete, continue with this final section, answering the posed questions as they are presented. (Note: This chapter has more questions throughout than the previous sections due to the critical process of setting goals.)

Making the Change

Honestly answer the following questions:

1. Acknowledging the goals you validated in the previous section; how will you sincerely consider and attempt each?

_____

_____

_____

_____

_____

2. Despite your perceived limitations, how do you believe you can accommodate them and still reach your goals?

_____

_____

_____

_____

_____

3. What "crazy ideas" have you had that you never set out to do?

_____

_____

_____

_____

_____

4. What current obstacles are in the way of you achieving these goals?

_____

_____

_____

_____

_____

Once you have crossed the threshold of "consideration" toward your goals and stepped into the "willingness" arena, it is time to commit to the process required for change. Before I ran my first marathon, I had to commit to training for a marathon. This meant I had to build up my endurance first to run 5 miles, then 10 miles, and eventually 20 miles before I could even consider running 26.2 miles.

The process of training for a marathon and the commitment to that process requires sacrifices. I found that I no longer could sleep in as I was accustomed to, and I needed to shed a few pounds to avoid making it more challenging than it already was! Additionally, I had to commit the time to making all of this happen.

As I have mentioned, all you control is your time and choices. Committing to the process is nothing more than controlling these two variables. When Jim Rohn suggested successful people do the things that unsuccessful people won't, he talked about the discipline of "making the right choices" and "committing the time to the process" that others are unwilling to.

Let's pause here for a time of reflection. To get this far in this book and your "Roadmap for Success," you have spent time discovering who you are (your Principles, Values, and Character) and have realized your continued purpose (reflecting on your life's experiences, observing the world around you, and seeing where you might fit in). Now, you are putting the "meat on the bones" of your "Roadmap for Success" by setting goals for continued growth in your golden years.

Discovering Joy in Your Golden Years revolves around realizing your goals, seeing the growth in "who you are" and your "Purpose," and knowing that you still have more to give and share in this life. This is why Shaq is still re-inventing himself in so many ways beyond the basketball court.

Here's a simple process for setting goals:

- Conceive your goals
- Write those goals down
- Review those goals frequently
- Create an action plan to achieve your goals

By crossing the finish line of your professional career, you have proven that you have the discipline to set goals and stick to a process for achieving them. You also realize only some of your goals will be achieved, but you know that many, if not most (85%), can be achieved. So, continuing to set retirement goals makes sense, which is why a commitment to the change process in retirement is an essential to making change.

Consider the following questions:

1. What does "committing to the process" of setting goals mean to you?

_____

_____

_____

_____

_____

2. What processes for reaching your goals worked well in the past?

_____

_____

_____

_____

_____

3. What "one thing" in your life has helped you realize your goals to date?

_____

_____

_____

_____

_____

4. What "one thing" in life has hindered you from achieving your goals in the past?

_____

_____

_____

_____

_____

Alexandria "Spiff" Sedrick is a 26-year-old Olympic Bronze Medal-winning USA Sevens Rugby Team member. Originally a multi-sport athlete in high school, she joined the women's rugby team when a volleyball teammate's sister introduced her to the game. After her first practice and getting tackled hard, she thought, this is not for me, but she just kept going back.

Setting goals and dreaming big led to an invite to the USA Sevens Residency and a debut in the World Rugby Sevens Series in 2021 for the Dubai Sevens. Three years later, she achieved Olympian status and was named to the Paris 2024 Team USA Roster. From being tackled hard and deciding this wasn't for her to scoring the last-minute goal to tie the match and kicking the winning extra point to secure the win, Spiff never stopped believing in her goals, the process, or the possibility. She exemplifies how believing in the results is the last and most important part of Making the Change.

I am convinced that the reason at least 85% of my past goals came to fruition is because I genuinely believed they could. By setting goals, reviewing them frequently, and making choices that aligned with those goals, I "believed" them into reality. The real credit goes to the power of our subconscious mind. When you commit to Making the Change by setting goals, committing to the process, and believing in the results, you activate your subconscious just by your habitual thought processes.

What you "plant" in your brain is no different than what is planted in rich soil; the law of sowing and reaping remains the same. In the same way, being deliberate about what you start your day with regarding what you think about and habitually thinking about it is also essential to your ability to grow and not stagnate. If you genuinely wish to make positive changes in your life, you must "feed" the subconscious with ideas and thoughts that are aligned with your growth aspirations to make these dreams a reality.

Consider the following questions:

1. What thoughts are consistently in your mind when you wake up?

_____

_____

_____

_____

_____

2. What experiences in your life have come about because you believed they could?

_____

_____

_____

_____

_____

3. If you were to list the three most important changes you would like to make in your golden years, what would they be?

_____

_____

_____

_____

_____

4. If you made these changes, how would they impact who you are, your continued purpose, and your impact in your sphere of influence?

_____

_____

_____

_____

_____

When you finish answering these questions in your journal, go back to the very beginning and take the time to read your current roadmap to date. Acknowledge who you are and who you have become in retirement, including since you started journaling. Ask yourself if there is anything missing in your answers. If so, add to or subtract from the list. Remember, becoming who you are is a never-ending journey. That is what makes your roadmap so valuable to you as you continuously review and revise it.

Now review your Continued Purpose statement to see if it accurately reflects where you see opportunities to "fill voids" in your sphere of influence. Have any new ideas come to mind since you last reviewed this section? If so, make the changes to ensure your continued purpose inspires and excites you as you approach this new phase of life. When you are satisfied with this section, move on to the section you just completed: Setting Goals for Continued Growth.

Review and reflect on the goals you have set in this section. Re-ask yourself if you can commit to reaching these goals. Are these goals aligned with your continued purpose and who you are? Do these goals inspire you and set the milestones in your roadmap to help you reach the Joy you are looking for in your Golden Years? If so, it's time to move on to the next chapter: **Realizing Your Potential by Wisely Investing Your Time and Choices.**

CHAPTER 4:

Realizing Your Potential by Wisely Investing Your Time and Choices

Tetra-Amelia syndrome (TETAMS) is a rare congenital disorder that causes the absence of all four limbs. It is a very rare disorder, affecting fewer than 1,000 people in the U.S. That is 1 in 333,300 people or .0003%! Contrast that with the fact that only 1.6% of all NCAA football players make the NFL, and only .03% make the pros in men's basketball.

Nick Vujicic has overcome TETAMS and become a global motivational speaker, spreading a message of hope and resilience to millions. He plays golf and swims, exemplifying the power of determination, adaptability, and a positive mindset to overcome perceived obstacles. I suspect that if he were asked if he has reached his full potential, he would remark in his Aussie accent, "Not yet, Mate, still working at it!"

Despite feelings of isolation, depression, and a lack of purpose, Nick Vujicic developed an inner courage that would mold his life to overcome the great hurdle of being born without arms or legs. His biggest effect has been as a motivational speaker, teaching optimism, perseverance, and the power of a positive mentality. He has motivated millions to overcome self-doubt and live a meaningful life through self-acceptance, accepting one's uniqueness, and overcoming hardships.

To reach the point where he could motivate "those with all four limbs," Nick Vujicic had to go through the process I have outlined so far in this book. He first had to accept himself (Discovering "Who" He Was), then accept his "uniqueness" (Realizing Continued Purpose), and finally overcome the mental and physical hardships of his rare disorder (Setting Goals for Continued Growth). He did this one step at a time by wisely investing his time and choices, striving to reach his full potential without really knowing what that might be.

As you approach the threshold of retirement, it is easy to look back on your career, family, and personal aspirations and question whether things turned out the way you planned. Retirement is too often viewed as the finish line instead of the chance to start a new once again! This is why your "Discover Joy in Your Golden Years Journal" is so important to making the most of your golden years. It will serve as your personal roadmap to starting new by focusing on the future instead of dwelling on the past.

Journal Chapter 4

"Realizing my Potential by Wisely Investing My Time and Choices"

Consider the following questions:

1. How will I achieve my potential in my golden years?

---

2. How will I use my time wisely to achieve my goals for con-tinued growth?

---

3. How will I ensure my choices are aligned with who I am and my purpose?

_____

_____

_____

_____

_____

4. What drives me to realize my potential?

_____

_____

_____

_____

_____

The answers to these four questions are foundational for realizing your potential in your golden years. Discovering who you are, realizing continued purpose, and setting goals for continued growth get you ready to take the first step toward realizing your potential, just as Nick Vujicic did without the advantage of arms and legs.

In previous chapters, I discussed the importance of controlling your time and choices to determine your purpose and committing to the process of continued growth by setting goals. Now, you are ready to move forward toward realizing your potential in these golden years and making the most of your time by **organizing for success**, aligning your choices to **choose wisely to control the things you can control**, and **believing in something bigger than yourself.**

<u>Organizing for Success</u>

Prior to the introduction of the shot clock in basketball, there was an offensive strategy known as the "four corners offense," which players used to retain a lead by holding on to the ball until the clock ran out. The strategy was for four players to go to each of the four corners of the offensive court. The remaining player, the point guard, would dribble the ball inside the four corners, hoping to draw the defense out and create a safe pass or guaranteed shot.

For the play to work, the team that used the four corners offense strategy would get the lead in the last few minutes of the game and then set up the four corners to run out the clock before the other team could score. While it's referred to as an offensive strategy, this, interestingly, was a defensive strategy. Teams that used it were holding onto what they had already achieved and simply waiting for time to expire.

Fortunately for the game of basketball, the shot clock was introduced, requiring players to take a shot within 24 seconds (NBA). When the time on the shot clock runs out, the other team gets the ball. This radically changed the game by getting teams to force the ball down the court, focusing on speed and offense the entire way. In fact, it changed the dynamics of the last few minutes to focus on winning instead of just holding the ball to not lose the game.

You might not be racing up and down a basketball court in your golden years, but the strategy of organizing for success during this phase in life is similar to what basketball players do. Instead of focusing on 24 seconds, you need to be deliberate about the 24 hours you are given each day. When you are no longer "on the clock" as in your previous profession (or perhaps "always on the clock" if you were an executive or leader), you will have to decide how you will make the most of your time. Will you choose the defensive approach of running out the clock, preserving all that you have accumulated and achieved to this point, or will you choose a purely offensive strategy to make the most of each day to ensure you have done everything you could have to fully realize your potential by the time the clock runs out?

By this point, you likely can surmise that I am encouraging you to take the latter approach. But I can't force you to take the ball down the court – you will have to make the first move. Newton's First Law of Motion states that a body at rest will remain at rest unless an outside force acts on it, and a body in motion at a constant velocity will remain in motion in a straight line unless acted upon by an outside force. You have been working on that "outside force" by creating your Discover Joy in Your Golden Years Journal and building your personal roadmap for "remaining in motion and in a straight line" in your golden years.

By knowing who you are, identifying your continued purpose, and establishing goals for continued growth, you can control your time to achieve your purpose and reach your goals for continued growth.

To realize your potential, you must be willing to grow beyond your current perceived limitations and learn how to get back up after you have fallen. You must believe in yourself, trust in your purpose, set goals to achieve growth, and then commit time each day to make your dreams a reality. In this context, create a new Journal Section titled "Organizing for Success."

<u>Organizing for Success</u>

Consider the following questions:

1. How much time do you require for a "good night's sleep?"

_____

_____

_____

_____

_____

2. How do you like to start your mornings?

3. How much time will you commit to your physical health daily?

4. How much time will you commit daily to achieving your growth goals?

5. How much time will you commit daily on your renewed purpose?

_____

_____

_____

_____

_____

6. How much time will you commit to your "me-time?"

_____

_____

_____

_____

_____

When Nick Vujicic decided to "take the first step" toward realizing his potential, he had to organize how he would use his time each day and commit to that plan. He certainly didn't just jump into the pool and start swimming or go to the driving range and start hitting golf balls. In fact, one of the hardest things he had to learn was "how to get back up after he had fallen down."

It is worth noting that you are in the "commitment" phase of your Journal to Discovering Joy in Your Golden Years. Think through your answers to each of these questions carefully, and ensure they are doable and sustainable. There will no doubt be occasions where your schedule will be interrupted by life, but you must be willing to commit to your daily plan as much as you can to realize your true potential.

When you have answered all the questions above and committed to those answers, take the time to go back through each section of your journal. Review your previous answers in the context of what you have just committed to. Edit and amend any of your previous answers as you see fit to ensure they are aligned with the commitments you have just made to yourself. If you realize any new voids you might be able to fill or new goals you would like to add for your growth, update as you see fit.

Once you are satisfied with your personalized roadmap, you will be ready to move on to the next section for realizing your potential: **Choose Wisely to Control the Things You Can Control**.

Choose Wisely to Control the Things You Can Control

On February 16, 1972, Air Force Lieutenant Ralph Galati, a flight navigator, was shot down in an F-4 Phantom jet over North Vietnam. Both he and his pilot safely ejected, parachuting into the center of an enemy village. After landing, they were immediately taken prisoner and moved to Hanoi. Galati would go on to endure 14 months of captivity, including interrogations, sleep and food deprivation, as well as 75 days in solitary confinement. Within mere seconds, his life changed from being in control of most of his circumstances to hardly being in control of anything.

In a May 2020 podcast, during the COVID pandemic, Ralph Galati shared some advice from his time in captivity to help others cope with their circumstances due to the pandemic. Here are a few of his comments:

• Understand and learn about your strengths and weaknesses
• Identify your internal and external resources
• Learn from others
• Ask: "What can I learn from this situation?"
• Return with Honor: Be true to yourself and your beliefs

The COVID pandemic reminded the world that everyone is a vulnerable and finite creature. In youth, it seemed like the "world was our oyster." You could do anything you wished or go anywhere you wanted to in life because you believed you had the ability to do so. As you got older, you realized there were limitations to what you could do and where you could go.

The pandemic brought this revelation to young and old alike, significantly changing perspective regardless of one's generation. Isolation, loneliness, and uncertainty replaced common gatherings, perceived acceptance, and relative certainty. Many felt forced to re-evaluate their circumstances and options. This is why Ralph Galati's advice was so relevant back then and continues to have applications for those considering retirement today.

Controlling the things you can control is all about deliberately choosing to understand your circumstances and, more importantly, the impact your choices have within those circumstances. Stephen Covey's quote, "Seek first to understand, then be understood," is so appropriate as you enter the golden years. In fact, everything you have done so far with your Discover Joy in Your Golden Years Journal has been about getting a new understanding of the role you will play in this new phase of life.

Knowing who you are, where you believe you best fit, and how you may achieve that by setting goals provides the fundamental understanding to achieving Joy in your golden years.

It is with that understanding that you embark on the quest to realize your potential by not only investing wisely with your time but also with your choices. Making choices that are aligned with your principles, values, and character will affirm who you are and help you realize your niche and continued purpose in life. Additionally, when you remain true to yourself with the choices that you make, you will realize your goals and continued growth in the golden years.

Let's look at a few choices you, like many people, may have made in the past and reflect on how they made you feel:

- Eating a hamburger and fries or a healthy salad

- Watching hours of the continuous news cycle or listening to music

- Spending hours in the recliner or getting physical exercise for one hour

- Sending text messages to friends and family or picking up the phone and talking directly

- Getting stressed by politics or seeking gratitude for the blessings you have

- Constantly reflecting on the failures of the past or rejoicing for the opportunities of the present

Hopefully, you can relate to this short list. It might even evoke some memories of how these dilemmas made you feel. Consider this sample list of feelings and attach those to the choices just described:

Energetic	Enthusiastic	Hopeful	Optimistic
Overwhelmed	Flustered	Confused	Fearful
Calm	Peaceful	Inspired	Trusting
Lonely	Frustrated	Depressed	Disappointed
Worried	Anxious	Panic	Scared
Enraged	Edgy	Irritated	Annoyed

Importantly, feelings are not the same as emotions. Emotions are immediate, instinctive responses to a situation or event, such as the feeling of fear you might get at the top of a roller coaster right before it drops. They are short-lived but intense. Feelings, in contrast, are your interpretation and internalization of your emotions. They are often fueled by emotions or a mixture of emotions. Mixing feelings together generates moods. While emotions last seconds to minutes, moods last minutes to hours. Therefore, if you find yourself in a "funky" or bad mood, it is worthwhile to consider any choices that led you to feel the mood you are experiencing.

Realizing the impact your choices can have on how you feel will not protect you from dealing with adversity and challenging times. You can't meditate your way out of a serious obstacle. Neither Ralph Galati nor Nick Vujicic was exempt; quite the contrary, they faced seemingly insurmountable odds. Yet, by choosing wisely, they conquered their circumstances and came out better for it. The lesson here is that the most significant single thing you can do to positively impact your golden years is to understand the impact of your choices during these culminating years.

The key to realizing your potential in your golden years is learning to get up when life knocks you down. Remember, getting up is a choice as well. Nick Vujicic could have easily decided that it was impossible to get up without any arms and legs. Yet, he chose to figure out how to use his forehead, neck muscles, core, and minor appendages to make the impossible possible. Similarly, to get up during your retirement years, you need to remain curious by constantly seeking to understand things you have yet to figure out and learning from those experiences. To avoid the rut of running out the clock in retirement, you must choose to step outside of your comfort zone and into new "growth opportunities." As Nick Vujicic says, "Often the very challenges that we think are holding us back are, in fact, making us stronger."

Staying just on this side of comfort means challenging yourself daily with something new. Learning a new language, learning how to cook, learning to play a new instrument, writing a book, painting a portrait, etc. are just a few ideas. When you choose to remain curious, there is no limit to what new things you may learn and further your potential. Just like taking a shot within the 24-second clock to keep the game moving, you need to take a shot every 24 hours to keep your life moving!

It's time to make an action plan. Create a new Journal Section titled: "Choosing Wisely" and answer the following questions. If you are like me, these are some tough questions to answer, so again, just let any answers flow from your stream of consciousness as if you were "brainstorming" with yourself and there are no bad answers. If you find yourself getting stuck, boldly go to your spouse, partner, or someone who knows you and ask for some insight.

Choosing Wisely

1. What choices am I currently making that are inconsistent with who I am?

_____

_____

_____

_____

_____

2. What choices do I make that are holding me back from realizing my potential?

_____

_____

_____

_____

3. What choices do I need to make to further my potential?

_____

_____

_____

_____

_____

4. What choices do I need to make to keep me just on this side of comfortable?

_____

_____

_____

_____

5. Do I frequently find myself in a "funk" or poor mood during the day?

_____

_____

_____

_____

6. What choices am I making that are contributing to the mood?

_____

_____

_____

Answering these questions will force you to be candidly introspective with yourself to identify the choices that are holding you back from realizing your potential. Keep in mind that humans are creatures of habit. You have had decades of building habits that work well for you and help you cope and get through the day. Habits are also choices and, at times, can be very difficult to break. As you consider your choices, also consider some of your habits to see if they are enhancing or detracting from growing and reaching your potential.

When you finish this brainstorming session with yourself and have answered all six questions, set your journal aside, find a quiet place, close your eyes, and reflect on this journey so far. Think about the anxiety you may have had previously as you considered your pending or current retirement. Reflect on what you have learned so far, who you are, your continued purpose, growth goals, and now time and choice commitments, and honestly assess how you feel.

Has any of your previous anxiety been replaced with excitement, confusion with clarity, or relevance with purpose? Take the time to assess where you are in this journey to Discovering Joy in Your Golden Years and your roadmap to date. When you are done with the personal assessment, it is time to address the final ingredient in realizing your potential: **Believing in Something Bigger than Yourself.**

Believing in Something Bigger Than Yourself

Oprah Winfrey self-proclaims that she grew up with stories of the bible before she learned nursery rhymes or fairy tales. In a groundbreaking seven-part series *Belief,* she shared how those bible stories taught her to believe in something bigger than herself. I especially appreciated her comment that "real fear was trusting in only myself" and that "being fearless was being able to release my fears to that which is greater than myself."

If you have ever met a United States Marine, you will discover that there is no such thing as an ex-Marine. Once a Marine, always a Marine. The incredibly rigorous training that transforms civilians to Marines instills the concept of being a part of something bigger than themselves. In fact, the Marine Corps motto since 1883, "Semper Fidelis," or Semper Fi, is "an eternal and collective commitment to the success of our battles, the progress of our Nation, and the steadfast loyalty to the fellow Marines we fight alongside."

Being a part of something bigger than yourself is the honest humility of acknowledging that life is not all about you; it is about the accountability of self to a higher cause, knowing that the higher cause also cares about you and your well-being. Nick Vujicic had faith that he was "fearfully and wonderfully made" to exist on this planet with a unique purpose, just like every other human being. He believed that "if it was meant to be," he could do it, so why not try? This mindset is the only thing that could have led to someone without any arms and legs learning how to swim and play golf.

Trusting in a higher purpose can push you forward when your faith in yourself wanes. Oprah said it best when she said the "real fear was in trusting in only myself." As you cross the threshold of your Golden Years, it is easy to say "I" have achieved all my professional goals, and "I" am ready to enjoy the fruits of my labor. But what if there is still potential to be realized beyond yourself? What if your entire life up to this point has prepared you for a time such as this? How will you ever know if you don't step out and try?

It's time to think beyond living for just yourself as you enter your retirement years. Create a new Journal Section titled "Believing in Something Bigger than Yourself" and answer the questions below.

Believing in Something Bigger than Yourself

1. Do you believe in something bigger than yourself? (If so, how would you describe it?)

_____

_____

_____

_____

_____

2. How have you had disappointments over the years when you had to completely rely on yourself?

_____

_____

_____

_____

_____

3. Who do you know that has demonstrated that "faith beyond self" and realized their potential through that faith?

_____

_____

_____

_____

_____

4. What are the benefits of believing in something bigger than yourself in realizing your potential?

_____

_____

_____

_____

_____

As you ponder your answers to the questions, I invite you to imagine the following possibilities. What if retirees just like you decided to explore their full potential in their Golden Years instead of running out the clock on the beach or the golf course? What if, by knowing who they are and who they could become, they had a renewed purpose to fill the voids within their spheres of influence and make a difference for future generations? What if they rejected the notion that retirement is nothing more than life's final buzzer and accepted the challenge to continue to grow to realize their full potential in life? What could this mean for society, community, government, and the world?

The answers lie in the realization that many of the things previously determined to be impossible are actually quite possible. The insurmountable is manageable, and the probability of finishing strong will increase exponentially as this previously untapped potential enters the equation. This leads us to our last Chapter, **Visualizing Your Lasting Impact: Personal and Relational.**

CHAPTER 5:

Visualizing Your Lasting Impact: Personal and Relational

I t was a crystal-clear blue-sky December day in Colorado. We would celebrate Christmas in three days, but this day was a celebration of life. Hundreds had gathered at Guardian Angel Catholic Church in Mead, Colorado. As I looked around the crowd, I recognized several family members and friends, mingling with a sea of unfamiliar faces.

We were celebrating the life of my mother, a third-grade school teacher who, as I mentioned earlier, departed this world at the young age of 50 due to cancer. The sound in the church was a mixture of sorrow and joy. Nearly everyone was conversing about a story where this ordinary woman had made them feel special—like they were the most important person on the planet.

During the reception, I was approached by many people I didn't know, and several who I did, who told me that my mother made a positive impact on their lives. How could this be? Most of them were middle-aged, so she wasn't their teacher. Many were affiliated with the school and community, but many were just casual acquaintances. I was perplexed and amazed at how my mother, a humble schoolteacher, had positively impacted hundreds of lives.

As I listened, it became obvious. You see, she made it her purpose to positively and purposefully engage in every relationship in her life. What is so ironic to me is that I didn't realize the impact that would have until we celebrated her life on that crystal-clear blue-sky December day! The common denominator in this room of hundreds of people was their relationship with my mother and the person she was in their lives.

We all carry the same potential to positively impact our communities and the lives of the people in them. You have come a long way in this journey to Discovering Joy in Your Golden Years and have documented your progress in a personal journal/ roadmap that will guide you toward making your golden years the best years of your life! It is time now to put it all together by visualizing the lasting impact you would like to make during these golden years, personally and relationally. Everything that has occurred in your life to this point has prepared you for just this time. The last section of your Discover Joy in Your Golden Years Journal will describe "your routine for success."

Just like the Olympian Stephen Nedoroscik visualizing his pommel horse routine before his successful medal performance, you are at the point where you need to visualize the culmination of "who you are, your continued purpose, goals for growth, and realizing your potential" to **determine your focus**: what you will wake up and go to bed thinking about, **acknowledge limitations**: making the most of each day despite challenges, **and following your "North Star"**: that inner sense or calling of what you want to accomplish in your life.

Determining Your Focus

Frank Siller has become the face of the Tunnel to Towers Foundation as both the Chairman/CEO and spokesman. The Siller family launched the Tunnel to Towers Foundation in 2002 to honor their Firefighter brother, Stephen Siller, who had just gotten off his shift on September 11, 2001. On his way home to meet his brothers for a round of golf, he heard that the planes hit the Twin Towers, so he turned his truck around, took his gear, and drove into the mouth of the Brooklyn Battery Tunnel to "rescue the rescuers."

When he got to the tunnel, traffic was at a standstill, so he strapped 60 lbs. of gear to his back and raced on foot through the tunnel to the Twin Towers, where he gave up his life while saving others. Stephen lived his life under the guiding philosophy of St. Francis of Assisi: "While we have time, let us do good." Frank Siller has made his brother's selfless actions and guiding philosophy the personal focus of the Tunnel to Towers

Foundation by helping the loved ones of fallen military and first responders with over 450 mortgage-free homes.

Everyone has events and milestones in their lives that force them to pause and evaluate what they are focused on. It could be the loss of a job, an unexpected illness, a death in the family, or a pending retirement. In each of these situations, it's important to reflect and ask yourself if you are making the most of your life—or, in St. Francis of Assisi's philosophy, doing the most good while you still have time.

The difference now is that you can focus on making the most of each day by acknowledging the present. You no longer have to focus on your professional career, raising a young family, accumulating wealth, or any of the typical "planning for the future" constraints you have already negotiated. Your golden years can be focused on making the most of the present and living each day to the fullest!

You are the "master of your destiny" and your quest to make the most of YOUR golden years personally and relationally. Just like stepping on the scale daily to determine if your diet is producing the results you are looking for, you can evaluate if your daily focus produces the results you desire in this exciting phase of life! Are you living true to yourself, realizing your continued purpose, achieving your goals for continued growth, and expanding your potential?

While seeing your weight on the scale move in your desired direction is good, it is even more meaningful when someone acknowledges your effort by telling you, "You look great!" The affirmation we get from others through their comments and expressions is priceless. This is why another facet of our daily focus has to be relational. By focusing each day on giving to those meaningful relationships in your life, you are investing in timeless impact. I saw first-hand the lasting impact of my mother's relational focus of committing each day to the relationships that were meaningful to her during her celebration of life.

It is now time to create another new Journal Section titled "Visualize Your Lasting Impact: Personal and Relational."

Journal Chapter 5

"Visualize Your Lasting Impact: Personal and Relational"

<u>My Daily Focus</u>

Consider the following questions:

1. What one word describes my personal focus in my Golden Years? *(Struggling? See some of my words on the next page)*

_____

_____

_____

_____

_____

2. How does this word capture who I am, my continued purpose, my goals for growth, and realizing my potential?

_____

_____

_____

_____

3. What one word describes my relational focus in my Golden Years?

_____

_____

_____

_____

_____

4. How does this word capture who I am, my continued purpose, my goals for growth, and realizing my potential?

_____

_____

_____

_____

_____

Coming up with a single word to answer questions one and
three might be challenging. Start by writing down any words
that come to mind. To help you out, here are some of the words
that come to my mind when I do the same:

Committed	Thankful	Challenged	Grateful
Uncertain	Fearless	Humbled	Selfless
Accountable	Responsible	Concerned	Honest
Reliable	Honored	Blessed	Trusting
Joyful	Amazed		

I acknowledge this is a little harder than the previous questions
you have considered, but remember, this is where you will start
each day. As you answer questions 2 and 4, reference each
completed section to validate the impact you desire for your
Daily Focus words.

As you develop the habit of starting each day with your focus
words, it will be beneficial to assess the impact your focus had at
the end of each day and then modify or adjust as required. To do

this, add a **"Daily Reflections"** section in the back half of your journal where you can write the date and answer the following questions on a daily basis:

- Did I live true to myself today: my principles, values, and character?

- Did I realize my continued purpose in doing the things I chose to do?

- Did I meet any of my goals for continued growth?

- Did I expand my potential for more?

As you end each day, reflect on these questions and assess your daily focus in terms of your answers. Based on this assessment, feel free to adjust or change your "one-word focus." This will allow you to further refine and enhance your daily impact in these Golden Years.

Additionally, as you reflect each day, you may find that there are some mental, physical, or vocational impediments keeping you from staying focused. Let's call these perceived limitations. To clearly visualize your impact in your Golden Years, you must have a daily focus and **Acknowledge Your Perceived Limitations** to refine that focus appropriately.

Acknowledge Limitations

Considered one of the mentally strongest humans on the planet, retired Navy Seal David Goggins has mastered the art of identifying and overcoming self-imposed limitations and limiting beliefs. Weighing over 300lbs, dyslexic, and unable to swim, Goggins changed his mentality from "can't" or "why" to "what" and "how."

Beginning with the mantra "failure is not an option," he realized there was more to just setting and relentlessly pursuing goals. He had to acknowledge his mental, physical, and vocational limitations to ensure he was "not the problem." For Goggins, it was as simple as answering two questions:

- What do I need to do to get this done?

- How do I push past this?

A quote from Goggins's best-selling audiobook, *Can't Hurt Me,* says it all when it comes to acknowledging and overcoming limitations: "You are in danger of living a life so comfortable and soft that you will die without ever realizing your true potential." As humans, we all have self-doubt and limiting beliefs about ourselves, our interactions, and our world. The reality is these beliefs are nothing more than assumptions we form based on our life experiences.

This is why daily self-assessments are invaluable to both discovering joy and realizing your true potential. Just as David Goggins transformed his mentality from "can't" or "why" to "what" and "how," it's important for you to transform your mentality to identify and acknowledge what is keeping you from moving forward. For example, when adversity or uncertainty strikes, instead of saying, "I can't believe this is happening," you could instead say, "What opportunities will this situation provide?"

Remember Nick Vujicic, the inspirational speaker born without arms and legs I mentioned in chapter 4? I suspect early on, he never thought he would be able to help himself up when he had fallen, let alone swim or play golf. Yet, once he accepted "what" and "how" for "can't" or "why," it transformed his life. Yes, you primarily use your arms and legs to swim, but what other muscles in your torso and core could do the same?

Remember, most of your limiting beliefs are assumptions based on life experiences. When life throws you a curve ball, and you know it will, start by acknowledging those assumptions/limitations and asking "what" and "how." Create a new section of your Journal titled "Acknowledge My Limitations: Personally and Relationally" and answer the questions from the following two scenarios. These tough yet very important questions will affirm who you are and help you realize your continued purpose.

Scenario 1: Personal Limitations

Country music star Toby Keith wrote a superb song about a conversation he had with actor, director, producer, and 94-year-old legend Clint Eastwood called "Don't Let the Old Man In." Keith asked Eastwood the secret to staying active and healthy at his advanced age. When you listen to the lyrics of this song (and I encourage you to do so), you will discover four central themes:

- Be deliberate about staying active and wanting to "Live me some more!"

- Make it a point to "get up and go outside" while you still can!

- Age is only a number and not a description or expectation: "How old would you be if you didn't know the day you were born?"

- Celebrate each day: None are promised, and all are gifts. "Toast each sundown."

Despite the physical, mental, and vocational limitations most 94-year-old men acknowledge and accept, Clint Eastwood decided in 1959 at the age of 29 to stay busy. In his words, he never let the old man in the house by living true to those four bullet points.

<u>Acknowledge My Limitations: Personally</u>

As you look at your personal limitations, consider the following:

1. What perceived personal limitations do you have that may keep you from realizing your full potential in your golden years?

_____

_____

_____

_____

2. What assumptions have you made for yourself in your golden years that may become limitations?

_____

_____

_____

_____

_____

3. How have you learned to be comfortable with the uncomfortable?

_____

_____

_____

_____

_____

4. What personal fears do you have in your golden years that may keep you from realizing your full potential?

_____

_____

_____

_____

_____

Scenario 2: Relational Limitations

Another country music star, Cody Johnson, sings the song "Til You Can't," which he claims has changed his life. This song talks about not missing relational opportunities and making the most of each day, as we have discussed throughout this book. Again, I encourage you to listen to the lyrics of this song as well, but here are four bullets that I believe sum up Cody's message:

- Don't put off until tomorrow what you can do today because tomorrow may never come: "Rainchecks" expire.

- Relationships need attention, or they will go dormant and fall away: "Further down the road" may be a dead end!

- The only way to realize your dreams is to chase them: "Cause a dream won't chase you back."

- Never take love for granted: "Hold 'em as long and as strong and as close as you can!"

The lyrics to this song describe many of the relational limitations you might believe stand in the way of meaningful relationships. It's easy to procrastinate and take rainchecks, assuming you will always have the chance to get together and work things out until, one day, you can't. Scientific research suggests that 85% of what we worry about never happens, and the 15% that does happen either provides a great learning lesson or could have been handled differently.[10] So, what are you actually afraid of?

If fear is holding you back from a meaningful relationship, take a chance and re-engage. You have an 85% chance for success! Even if you fail, you may learn a meaningful lesson or devise a different approach. Don't wait "Til you can't!"

---

10 Nalley, S. (2021, Jun 18), Getting Past Self Imposed Limitations and Limiting Beliefs. *Relentless Pursuit Magazine*. https://medium.com/pursuit-magazine/getting -past-self-imposed-limitations-and-limiting beliefs-fc4a3399306

Acknowledge My Limitations: Relationally

Consider the following questions:

1. What relationships are you holding back on that you could step out on and move forward?

2. What relational limitations keep you from realizing the impact you desire in your Golden Years?

3. What assumptions have you accepted that may keep you from realizing your potential relationally?

Discover Joy in Your Golden Years

4. Where have you been procrastinating on relationships that you may regret in the future?

_____

_____

_____

_____

_____

Remember, these limitations are what you perceive based on your life experiences. Just as David Goggins did in his life, you must now challenge these limitations to ensure you are not in your own way. If so, you can re-think your approach and start getting comfortable with what was uncomfortable. To truly have clarity when visualizing your impact in the Golden Years, you need to have clarity of focus and an acknowledgment of limitations and follow your heart and what guides your heart, **Your True North.**

Follow Your True North

President Ronald Reagan was the President of the Screen Actors Guild and a leading man in several motion pictures before becoming a political candidate at 55. While he enjoyed his Hollywood life, it was becoming increasingly difficult to live true to his principles, values, and character as the movie industry was being drawn into world politics that were inconsistent with his American values.

Despite believing he was in the industry he was meant to be in, this discomfort was becoming increasingly prevalent, and it became clear that he needed to follow his heart and make a difference elsewhere. Ronald Reagan realized that his True North was his undying belief in the inherent goodness of the American people and way of life. Elected governor of California as a conservative Republican for two terms, Reagan still felt that there was more to be done to preserve our American values, and he was determined to do just that.

By following his True North, Ronald Reagan realized that the place where he could make the greatest difference was as the President of the United States, even if he was 65 years old and many of his contemporaries were enjoying retirement. It would take him two times to finally be elected to the highest office in the land, and he would be the oldest person (at the time) elected president at the age of 69.

Your True North is the culmination of knowing who you are, realizing your purpose, setting goals for personal growth, believing in your potential to make a difference, and then visualizing or believing it can happen. Ironically, it takes most of our lives to finally settle in on our True North. We live most of our lives conforming to someone else's policies and procedures without taking the time to know who we really are and what is important to us. Additionally, we often held back how we really felt about something, fearing others would not understand.

Look at this list of the five common regrets people have at the end of their lives:

- I wish I had the courage to live a life true to myself, not the life others expected.

- I wish I hadn't worked so hard.

- I wish I'd had the courage to express my feelings.

- I wish I had stayed in touch with my friends.

- I wish that I had let myself be happier.

Do any of these common regrets resonate with you? Have you heard them before from your peers, relatives, or friends? What can you do to ensure that you do not have these regrets later in life?

Different for every person, your True North is a combination of your values, beliefs, and purpose. It is that inner sense, or calling, of what you want to accomplish in your life. In summary, it consolidates everything you have written in your Discover Joy in Your Golden Years Journal to date! Take the time now to carefully go through your journal and review your answers to each of the questions posed.

As you review each of your answers, ask yourself the following:

- Do I have a clear picture of who I am and what is important to me and guides me?

- Do I have a clear sense of my purpose for my Golden Years?

- Have I set realistic and attainable goals for growth in my Golden Years?

- Do I have an attainable plan for wisely using my time and making choices?

- Have I narrowed down a clear daily focus to move me toward realizing my full potential?

Note that this is the first time I have posed YES/NO questions, and this is deliberate. The roadmap you have developed to Discover Joy in Your Golden Years is uniquely tailored to you and your individuality. The previous five questions are designed to ensure you have the detail and clarity to make this roadmap a reality.

After reviewing your roadmap and validating the details and clarity, it is time to discover your True North. Create a new Journal Section titled "My True North" and answer the following questions:

My True North

1. Based on your review of your personal roadmap to Discover Joy in Your Golden Years, what do you believe is your calling?

_____

_____

_____

_____

_____

2. Based on your review of your personal roadmap to Discover Joy in Your Golden Years, what do you have left to accomplish?

_____

_____

_____

_____

3. As you consider your calling and purpose, what is guiding you toward that True North?

_____

_____

_____

_____

<u>Bringing it All Together</u>

Now that you have documented your Personal and Relational Focuses, Acknowledged Limitations, and identified Your True North, let's bring all of that together to identify specific impact areas both Personally and Relationally. How would you fill in the blanks in the following Impact Statement?

"Based on a clear understanding of who I am, my realized purpose, my commitment to continued growth, and realizing my full potential by wisely investing in my time and choices, I believe I can significantly impact the following areas of my life personally and relationally.

Personal

1. _____

2. _____

3. _____

4. _____

5. _____

6. _____

Relational

1. _____

2. _____

3. _____

4. _____

5. _____

6. _____

Remember where we started in this chapter about the celebration of life and my mother's impact on each of those in attendance? Some said she made them feel like the most important person in the room, that she was sincerely involved in their lives, that she always had time for them, that she always had a kind smile, that she was always there when they needed her, that she was their best friend.

All these responses (and there were many more) were genuine and sincere. As I mentioned before, you may never truly know the impact you will have on others, but they will never forget! Continue using your journal to dig deeper into the many ways you can continue to have a lasting impact on the people and world around you.

Some Final Thoughts

I magine waking up each day in your golden years with a clear understanding of who you are, what is important to you, a real sense of purpose, and the motivation to continue challenging yourself with growth opportunities. By completing this book and, more importantly, your Discover Joy in Your Golden Years Journal, you now have a personalized roadmap to realize just that! From this point on, you can actively chart your path in retirement by using the three "Rs": Reflect, Respond, and Rejoice.

Reflect

Peyton Manning became one of the greatest NFL quarterbacks of all time not because he was one of the most gifted athletes (although he clearly was gifted), but because he had an unquenchable thirst for feedback and reflection. When other players were enjoying a little time off, Peyton was reviewing films, reflecting on past performances, and visualizing his next outing. His habit of daily reflection created momentum for perpetual growth in Peyton's career and led him through the remarkable success he enjoyed in the NFL.

You might not be a professional football player, but that doesn't mean you can't train like one. The habit of finishing each day by answering the Daily Reflection questions in your journal can provide the same perpetual growth during your retirement. As a reminder, here they are:

- Did I live true to myself today: my principles, values, and character?

- Did I realize my continued purpose in doing the things I chose to do?

- Did I meet any of my goals for continued growth?

- Did I expand my potential for more?

Writing candid and honest responses to these questions will allow you to end each day with concrete details to support tomorrow's game plan.

Just as in your professional life, there will be days of success and days of failure during retirement. It's part of the human experience. Nick Vujicic did not become adept at swimming and golfing overnight. Once he accepted who he was and his new purpose in life, he had to learn how to get up when he fell. Without any arms and legs, it would have seemed impossible, but by learning from his failed attempts and visualizing a new approach, he eventually mastered getting back up when life knocks you down. Now, he models and inspires all of those within his sphere of influence. You can do the same!

Remember that it's not about how many times you fall down; it's about what you do next. This is a lesson I tried to impart to my children. Like most dads, I enjoyed regaling stories of my youth to my kids as they grew up. They tuned me out some of the time. But their ears perked up when I told a story where I had made a mistake and failed at something. It wasn't just that they liked hearing that their dad was less than superhuman (although that may have been part of it); what they really enjoyed hearing was what I had done in response to situations that didn't go my way.

In the same way, you need to decide what you will do when you fall down. This leads us to the second important "R" to charting our path in retirement, "Respond."

Respond

The renowned Greek teacher Epictetus is often quoted as saying, "It's not what happens to you, but how you react to it that matters." By taking the time each night to accurately reflect on the day, you are making notes for how you will address the day that follows. To realize your full potential in your golden years, you need to view any shortcomings from the previous day as unique opportunities for real growth, both personally and relationally.

Therefore, start each new day by reviewing your notes from the previous night to set your mindset for the rest of the day. You'll want to continue repeating things that went well and focus on improving on the things that went less than great—those are the real gems, the moments you will respond to by consciously acting out your retirement roadmap.

Building your daily game plan based on your reflections on areas of improvement from the previous day will help you grow personally. It will also help you grow relationally. Undoubtedly, there is someone in your life who would benefit from learning how you dealt with a particular circumstance. By sharing your humanity and telling the story of how you overcame a setback or failure, you are not only showing them how you grew from that experience and how they could possibly do the same, but you are also strengthening your relationship as you demonstrate vulnerability with them.

You see, it is not so much what has happened to us in life that is meaningful, but rather our response that gives meaning to our lives and the lives of others. When we make it our mission to continue to grow both personally and relationally through daily reflection and a determined response, we can realize a lasting impact and rejoice, which is the third "R" in charting our retirement path.

<u>Rejoice</u>

As you see personal and relational growth, you will realize a pure relevance to yourself by living true to who you are, as well as a relevance to those around you as you impact their lives with your time and choices. Perhaps without cognitively knowing it, you will feel joy surrounding you and peace in knowing you still matter!

Each day will be a gift for more growth and impact, knowing there is still so much to give and do to realize your continued purpose. Utilizing your Discover Joy in Your Golden Years Journal daily will keep you on this path of rejoicing in all circumstances and give you the opportunity to spread that joy throughout your sphere of influence. Finally, the living document you have created will also serve as a memoir of your golden years, sharing insight into your journey of personal growth and continued purpose that will encourage and guide your loved ones to do the same. In a sense, this Journal could be your written legacy.

I want to personally commend you on completing your journal/ roadmap and embarking on a journey that will bring you joy and fulfillment!

Call To Action

As the next step in your journey and an added benefit and commitment to your success, I invite you to send me a copy of your "Who I have become statement", "My Continued Purpose statement," and the answers to "My True North" questions to my email: *rphillips@c2eusa.com*. I will then schedule you for a complimentary 1-hour session to discuss the alignment of your roadmap with your identity, purpose, and goals to ensure your ultimate vision becomes a reality in your golden years.

I look forward to answering any questions you may have about how to make your Discover Joy in Your Golden Years Journal more effective to ensure your golden years are the best years of your life. Additionally, as I mentioned early in the book, I have set up a process with the publisher to create a personalized Discover Joy in Retirement Journal that could be a memoir for you and your family members for years to come. If you are interested in that, I will be happy to discuss it with you.

Now, as you cross the threshold into this amazing phase of your life, know that you will always have an advocate who is there to ensure your success. I am so excited for you and your journey, and I wish you the very best!

Use this part of your journal to answer the questions below daily:

"Daily Reflections"

Date: _____

- Did I live true to myself today: my principles, values, and character?

_____

_____

_____

_____

- Did I realize my continued purpose in doing the things I chose to do?

_____

_____

_____

_____

- Did I meet any of my goals for continued growth?

_____

_____

_____

_____

- Did I expand my potential for more?

_____

_____

_____

_____

_____

Date: _____

- Did I live true to myself today: my principles, values, and character?

_____

_____

_____

_____

- Did I realize my continued purpose in doing the things I chose to do?

_____

_____

_____

_____

- Did I meet any of my goals for continued growth?

_____

_____

_____

_____

_____

- Did I expand my potential for more?

_____

_____

_____

_____

_____

Date: _____

- Did I live true to myself today: my principles, values, and character?

_____

_____

_____

_____

- Did I realize my continued purpose in doing the things I chose to do?

_____

_____

_____

_____

_____

- Did I meet any of my goals for continued growth?

_____

_____

_____

_____

- Did I expand my potential for more?

_____

_____

_____

_____

Date: _____

- Did I live true to myself today: my principles, values, and character?

_____

_____

_____

_____

_____

- Did I realize my continued purpose in doing the things I chose to do?

_____

_____

_____

_____

_____

- Did I meet any of my goals for continued growth?

_____

_____

_____

_____

_____

- Did I expand my potential for more?

_____

_____

_____

_____

_____

Date: _____

- Did I live true to myself today: my principles, values, and character?

_____

_____

_____

_____

- Did I realize my continued purpose in doing the things I chose to do?

_____

_____

_____

_____

- Did I meet any of my goals for continued growth?

_____

_____

_____

_____

_____

- Did I expand my potential for more?

_____

_____

_____

_____

_____

www.ingramcontent.com/pod-product-compliance
Lightning Source LLC
Chambersburg PA
CBHW072203090426
42740CB00012B/2376